Cost Management in the New Manufacturing Age

Cost Management in the New Manufacturing Age

Innovations in the Japanese Automotive Industry

Yasuhiro Monden

Foreword by
Brian H. Maskell

Publisher's Message by
Norman Bodek
President, Productivity, Inc.

Productivity Press
Cambridge, Massachusetts   Norwalk, Connecticut

Productivity Press
P.O. Box 3007
Cambridge, Massachusetts 02140
United States of America
Telephone: (617) 497-5146
Telefax: (617) 868-3524

Cover design by Joyce C. Weston
Printed and bound by Maple-Vail Book Manufacturing Group
Printed in the United States of America

Grateful acknowledgment is made to the following for
permission to reprint previously published material:

Institute of Industrial Engineering:
For "Toyota Cost Management System in Japanese Automobile Corporations" and "Framework of the Just-In-Time System." Full credit listed in text.
Journal of Business Administration (University of British Columbia):
For "Full Cost-based Transfer Pricing in the Japanese Auto Industry: Risk-sharing and Risk-spreading Behavior" by Yasuhiro Monden and Teruya Nagao (Vol. 17, No. 1 & 2, 1987-88, pp. 117-136).
Kigyo kaikei (Business Accounting Journal), 40, No. 5 (1988).

Library of Congress Cataloging-in-Publication Data

Monden, Yashuhiro, 1940-
    Cost management in the new manufacturing age: innovations in the Japanese automotive industry/Yashuhiro Monden
        p.   cm.
    Includes bibliographical references and index.
    ISBN 0-915299-90-9
    1. Automobile industry and trade—Japan— Cost control.   I. Title.
HD9710.J32M66 1992   91-30805
629.2'068'1--dc20   CIP

92 93 94 10 9 8 7 6 5 4 3 2 1

Contents

Illustrations

Publisher's Message

A revolution is occurring in today's manufacturing environment. Production systems geared for success are evolving toward one-piece flow. This is a drastic change from the previous realm of mass production. And this change is occurring either naturally — or under duress — because it cannot be avoided. My point here is that if we change the way we think about production, we likewise must change the way we think about accounting and financial measures.

Because of a lack of understanding about production, the people in controller's offices often construct some of the most difficult bottlenecks while thinking they are on the road to achieving world class excellence. By better understanding production, however, they might actually improve their internal customer service. These days, in fact, people in our financial departments will learn a lot about innovation and creativity by spending some time on the plant floor. Valuable lessons can be applied to white-collar productivity. Chief among these may be how to reduce cycle time. After all, a process is a process is a process.

This new understanding cannot be separated from the highly competitive worldwide manufacturing environment. Today, if manufacturers are not modifying their current methods of cost management to respond to the changes in manufacturing, I guarantee that they won't be around in the new century. It is for this reason that I publish books such as *Cost Management in the New Manufacturing Age: Innovations in the Japanese Automotive Industry* by Yasuhiro Monden.

I first met Professor Monden in 1980 when he was a visiting professor of accounting at the State University of New York in Buffalo. He was one of the first academics from either side of the Pacific to talk with authority about the new Japanese manufacturing mentality. At that time, I asked him for two things: (1) for information on the new manufacturing techniques to publish in our monthly "Productivity" newsletter and (2) to address an upcoming Productivity seminar. He agreed. He sent us material on the concepts of just-in-time (JIT) production and *kanban*, which were first published in the United States in our newsletter. And in 1981, he spoke along with Professor Robert W. Hall, professor of operations management at Indiana University, at our Chicago seminar.

His clear perspective of the Toyota production system impressed me. He spoke with the full cooperation of Taiichi Ohno, then vice president of Toyota Motors Corporation. Professor Monden was the first person in America to discuss these concepts. In this book he continues to bring greater clarity to this revolution in manufacturing. In a single volume, he pulls together his understanding of the cost accounting, cost control, and cost planning methods used in Japan's auto industry — the leading proponent of world class manufacturing and JIT production methods.

Ten chapters contain the accumulated material of over a decade of study in this area. In Chapter 1, the author opens his discussion. In Chapter 2, he explains cost accounting and cost control as it relates to financial accounting and looks at cost planning at Toyota.

Nearly every company in the Toyota Group has completed implementing the total cost management system under the guidance of Toyota Motors. Toyota considers the system capable of horizontally governing the cost management of multiple departments; it is of great significance in what Toyota calls "functional management." Chapter 3 examines this approach. Many Japanese manufacturers have implemented it and broken down their cost management departments into cost control, cost planning, and cost improvement sections.

Chapter 4 presents the framework of the JIT production system. The aim of the Toyota production system is to increase profits by reducing costs — that is, by completely eliminating waste such as excessive inventory or workforce. The concept of costs in this context is broad. It is essentially the past, present, or future cash outlay deducted from sales revenue to attain a profit. Therefore, costs include not only manufacturing costs (reduced by cutting the workforce), but also administrative, capital (reduced by inventory cuts), and sales costs. To achieve cost reduction, production must promptly and flexibly adapt to changes in market demand without having waste. This ideal is accomplished through JIT production — producing needed goods in the needed quantities when they are needed.

In Chapter 5, Professor Monden discusses the relationship between the JIT system and cost accounting/control, a relationship that has been the topic of numerous case studies published in North America. The author presents a case study of Daihatsu Motor Company and makes some observations on how its cost accounting/control systems have developed under the JIT production system.

Chapter 6 concentrates on materials requirement planning (MRP) and examines systems that integrate it with the kanban method and the cost accounting system. The development of computer-assisted decision-making support systems is happening so quickly in the fields of production control and cost accounting that major changes appear almost monthly. Standard cost accounting systems developed on the basis of computer techniques for production control include those like MRP developed in the United States.

Production control techniques noted for their Japanese characteristics include the Toyota production control and *kanban* methods. Kanban, a Japanese word for signboard or card, also refers to the system utilizing standard containers, each of which has a card designating what and when to produce. (For further reading, see *Kanban and Just-In-Time at Toyota: Management Begins at the Workplace* [Cambridge MA: Productivity Press, 1989].) Although the use of computers is indispensable for the kanban method, it is not in opposition to MRP. In Japan many companies use both methods simultaneously.

time in case of model changes. During the first year, the concept of the new model is determined in meetings held with the marketing staff. The next seven to ten months sees the preparation for production. During the next year, a stage is reached when a design concept of a new model is further developed, a target cost is assigned to it, and details are worked out regarding design and cost requirements.

Chapter 8 explains how cost accounting systems and profit management systems are being applied in the Japanese automobile industry. Until recently, cost accounting was done according to the textbook. We could say, in fact, that the textbook model for cost accounting was to simplify calculating the real cost of individual products. This chapter, however, explains standard cost accounting within the current changing production and sales environments.

Chapter 9 describes the risk-sharing and risk-spreading behavior found between producers of finished autos and producers of auto parts in Japan. It shows how the auto maker seeks to motivate the parts manufacturer's commitment to invest in necessary parts production for new car models through risk- sharing arrangements. In analyzing risk management, it focuses on the parts transfer-pricing scheme between automobile and parts manufacturers.

Chapter 10 discusses the economic efficiency of accounting, emphasizing decisions that pertain to factory automation (FA) while attempting to define present approaches of Japanese automobile manufacturers toward the progress of factory automation. Although FA has a number of objectives, its most important aim is economic efficiency, expressed as increased productivity and reduced costs. The extent of FA development in Japan is clarified in another case study of Daihatsu.

I hope you feel compelled to read this book — even if you are not an auto maker — because all of us involved in manufacturing have the need to know. Only then can we customize the new methodologies to suit our own particular situations. Successful U.S. examples are already emerging. For instance, Quantum Medical Systems, Inc., a medical equipment manufacturer, wanted a simple inexpensive accounting system to focus on value-adding activities and dovetail with its JIT production system. To that end, it began utilizing several new accounting measures including (1) a monthly output rate, which measures total process efficiency; (2) inventory turns, which give management a measure of inventory movement per level of sales; and (3) hours per unit, which shows how well production workers are learning their own jobs and those of others.

Eaton Corporation's Power Distribution Division in Lincoln, Illinois, formed a cross-functional task force in 1988 to overhaul business and manufacturing processes. According to Controller Al Houser, they wanted to streamline their manufacturing operations and simplify their accounting and reporting systems.

Accounting systems usually end up matching the physical production flow. Previously, with lots of inventory and work-in-process (WIP), Eaton's accountants tracked numerous WIP accounts and intermediate transactions. Now production proceeds from start to finish in one continuous flow. The only things reported today are receipt of purchased parts (in order to pay bills and update inventory) and the shipments that relieve inventory. Houser insists that in a continuous flow environment devoid of WIP, you only need to report products that ship — your computer can then backflush the material. Backflushing eliminates a lot of needless paperwork and reduces opportunities for error.

I could go on. These examples, however, should give you a taste for the innovative ideas that may inspire you and your colleagues by reading from Professor Monden's experiences. I extend my heartfelt thanks to the author for permitting us to publish another of his fine books. I also thank the many people who made this project possible, among them Stephen Vitek, translator; Susan Cobb, project manager, and the production team of Katie Sweeney and Michele Saar; Cheryl Rosen, acquisitions and project editor; Dorothy Lohmann, managing editor; Bill Berling, freelance copyeditor; Joyce Weston, cover design.

Norman Bodek
President
Productivity, Inc.

Foreword

It is good to know that, as Western manufacturers, we have come through the period of glib explanations for the "Japanese miracle" and are now beginning to examine the issues more deeply. Our first response in the 1970s, when Japanese manufacturers began to seriously attack our markets and profitability, was to deny that these new competitors represented any long-term threat. Many Western companies — either from inertia, hubris, or lack of understanding — did not take any radical action to ensure their continued market share, profits, or, indeed, survival.

It soon became clear, however, that some of the new Japanese companies did present a real threat because their design, quality, price, and service were just plain better. What astonished many of us was their quality. We had been raised and trained with a rejection-rate mentality; the concept of zero defects was unbelievable. Other companies were dumbfounded by price. Xerox Corporation, as a part of its initial competitive benchmarking analysis in 1982, was shocked rigid to discover that Japanese competitors were selling equivalent copiers for less than the Xerox manufacturing cost.

The realization that prominent Japanese companies were in many ways superior led to the search for the secret of their success. The result of this search has been the realization that there is no single secret. These manufacturers have been extremely innovative in gradually unshackling themselves from traditional manufacturing ideas, and have cut to the core of issues like quality, cycle time, employee involvement, customer needs, and market share. The truth of the matter is that their success has been built on innovative change throughout the entire organization. If we are looking for a new technique or a "quick fix," we look in vain. There are no quick fixes.

We have now moved into a new era where we recognize that to be world class manufacturers we have to be ready to examine, change, and rethink every aspect of our businesses. There are, of course, many Western companies that have been most successful at meeting this challenge from the Pacific Rim. Not just imitators, either; but nimble organizations that have displayed enormous skill in restructuring from the top down and putting innovative approaches into place. These companies are truly world class.

Most Western companies, even the good ones, have found it difficult to make changes to their cost accounting and performance measurement systems. These systems are well entrenched in tradition, accepted accounting practice, and the corporate power structures. Yet the way a company measures and controls itself is at the heart of its ability to adapt and innovate. Yasuhiro Monden's book *Cost Management in the New Manufacturing Age* is rightly subtitled *Innovations in the Japanese Automotive Industry* because it lucidly presents the radical rethinking of management accounting through the eyes of some of Japan's best automotive companies.

The principles and practices of management accounting in leading Japanese companies are now thoroughly different from those of the United States and Western Europe. We would do well to take note not only of the techniques described in this book, but also of the role and position of the cost accountant in the design process, decision support, and control of these companies. There is a quiet revolution going on here and we need to come to grips with it. There are some aspects that can be readily integrated into Western management accounting — target costing and value engineering, for example — while others need to be adapted and revised by innovative Western companies.

Professor Monden is particularly helpful in showing the relationship between cost management and the techniques of kanban and MRP; this has long been a topic for conjecture, conflict, and confusion. The case studies dealing with the applications of cost planning, standard costing, and risk sharing provide valuable insight while striking the right balance between the academic and the practical.

One of our major challenges over the next few years (and one that most companies have so far neglected) is the rethinking of the methods and role of management accounting in manufacturing companies, particularly in the areas of cost planning, cost control, performance measurement, and capital investment. I enthusiastically commend this book to your attention.

Brian H. Maskell

Preface

The aim of this book is to explain cost accounting, cost control, and cost planning methods used in the Japanese automobile industry.

In recent years, diversification and the development of new products has been necessitated by the needs of the market. In addition, the just-in-time (JIT) production method has become the most widely used production method in the Japanese automobile industry. Computer technology has become incorporated into many aspects of production — influencing the utilization of machines as well as production planning. The question that needs asking is how methods of cost management have been modified in response to these changes in the manufacturing environment.

First of all, "cost planning" has become an important element of product planning and design. The development of a target costs design is achieved through value engineering (VE) based on target costs derived from target profits for new products. The process is verified by cost estimating.

Next, in order to improve the methods of JIT accounting, "cost control" has been employed through a method that we can call "cost improvement." A cost reduction range is assigned in the form of "a cost improvement amount" in order to reach periodic target profits in production facilities for existing products. These targets are set at each level of the internal organizational structure of the production facility. This provides control over the material aspects of each area of production, while at the same time ensuring influence over the accounting process by measuring the amount of cost improvement. In terms of cost accounting methods, an additional problem has been the utilization of MRP databases derived from production planning methods based on computer-integrated manufacturing (CIM), and how to allocate processing expenses and calculate economic efficiency based on CIM.

Thus, to understand the status of cost management in the leading Japanese automobile industries, it is important to analyze not only the automobile corporations but other production areas as well.

No textbook in the world provides a standardized explanation of the new methods of cost management that are based on the new manufacturing environment. That is what makes the challenge posed by the research and analysis that must be conducted at this stage so formidable. And this is why I have studied the actual conditions and techniques as they have been introduced in some of Japan's leading automobile corporations.

When analyzing actual conditions in the Japanese automobile industry I was particularly fortunate to obtain the cooperation of Mr. Goro Ito, Mr. Hitoshi Sumi, and Mr. Takashi Ishidera from Toyota Motor Corporation; of Mr. Yoshiteru Noboru, Mr. Shigeyoshi Takagi, Mr. Yoshiaki Fukamori, and Mr. Teruhiko Yoshihara from the Daihatsu Motor Company, Ltd.; of Mr. Toshiaki Okada and Mr. Yuji Yamaguchi from the Kubota Company, Ltd.; and of others as well. I am very grateful to these busy men for cordially receiving me and answering my questions. I express my gratitude from the bottom of my heart and I wish them continued success in their work.

Finally, I wish to thank Mr. Steven Ott, vice president of Productivity Press, and Ms. Cheryl Rosen, acquisitions and project editor, for their efforts in publishing this book in the United States.

1

Introduction

We can characterize the contemporary manufacturing environment in Japan by changes in three areas. First, it has diversified in response to market needs, resulting in the production of smaller quantities of a wider variety of products. Second, the just-in-time (JIT) production management system has been widely introduced. Third, progress in technology has resulted in automation and the extensive use of computer-integrated manufacturing systems (CIM).

Textbooks have yet to explain the new cost management systems and price calculations corresponding to these changes in the production environment. Therefore, the task of academics must be to explain the actual conditions existing in the best companies in Japan. In other words, case studies of cost accounting and management systems are required to construct new guidelines for the calculation of costs and systematization of a new system of cost control. That is why this study makes use of surveys and interviews with people in Japanese automobile corporations, the leading companies in Japan's production sector. Based on the changes mentioned previously, these case studies illustrate the kind of changes required in current cost management and accounting systems. The following sections provide an outline of the study and explain the changes according to current cost management techniques.

Small-Lot Production and Planning Current Costs in Response to Diversifying Market Needs. At present, it is important for corporations to be able to produce goods quickly at a low cost that will satisfy customers. The reason for this is that, together with the tendency toward diversification, the life cycle of individual products has been shortened. Under these circumstances, methods of cost reduction are used as cost management methods. These methods also include product planning and design activities. Such a system includes: (1) planning products that satisfy the needs of the customers; and (2) determining a target cost of these products that necessitates a value engineering (VE) process in addition to a design process.

Each company of the Toyota Group has developed a similar cost planning system under the guidelines of the Toyota Motor Corporation. Having examined case studies of cost planning systems in the Toyota Group, I have divided cost planning roughly into two stages — overall planning and cost planning in a narrow sense.

The overall planning stage entails the development of a long-term general profit plan. During this stage, the target profit is established for each of the main products based on planned investment in equipment, personnel, and individual structural plans. These target profits are allocated to each of the projects planned by new product development and represent targets that must be achieved through cost planning activities.

The second stage, cost planning in a narrow sense, encompasses cost reduction planning that is divided into cost management and cost control. Cost planning can be broadly classified as consisting of two processes. These processes are: (1) the concrete planning of products that satisfy customer needs and processes that introduce target prices from target profits of these new products, and (2) a process of verification through real cost estimates of these target prices, achieved by applying value engineering (VE) to drafted plans.

The Just-In-Time Production System and Its Relationship to Cost Management and Cost Accounting. Developed by Toyota, the just-in-time production system is now being adapted to manufacturers around the world. Based on the JIT production system, cost management proper is implemented under the direct effect of cost influencing factors. That is why the calculation of target costs and similar methods of accounting and cost management seem to be in retreat. In other words, physical target management systems are being applied based on present JIT management methods. This also means that financial management, together with accounting management and control systems, are still important. Since I am convinced that targeting control over both amounts of money and management systems will remain unchanged, this study examines various forms of implementation of cost management through JIT within the framework of managerial accounting.

The Relationship between CIM, Cost Management, and Cost Accounting. Roughly defined, computer-integrated manufacturing (CIM) is an integrated system consisting of three important components:

1. *Computer-aided design (CAD):* This term includes CAD proper — a manufacturing design technique — as well as other techniques, ranging from layout design to process design.
2. *Computer-aided manufacturing (CAM):* This term refers to the mechanical processing and the assembly of parts, when processing is automatically implemented and parts are assembled according to the commands of a host computer.
3. *Computer-aided planning (CAP):* This term encompasses techniques of production planning and scheduling using order-entry systems and market research planning.

Although all of these techniques are based on methods that have been developed in the United States, they have spread quickly throughout Japan in recent years.

CIM's primary aim is to create a flexible system that can adapt to changes in types and quantities of products manufactured for the market (that is, a system with a short lead time). The term "lead time" used in this book includes time required for demand analysis, as well as equipment design, mechanical processing and assembly, and the distribution of products.

I have conducted case studies and theoretical research while investigating similar CIM techniques — in particular, research of computer-aided design techniques such as order-entry systems and production planning with market research planning. This book is an attempt to establish whether or not a production planning database that uses MRP can be used as a means of cost accounting.

Together with the introduction of robots and other advanced equipment used in today's automobile industry, the calculation of real costs has changed. Specifically, it has changed with respect to the distribution of indirect costs. For these reasons, it will be necessary to study in further detail a whole range of procedures, from real economic calculations to function analysis design procedures, topics that will be examined in subsequent chapters.

2

Cost Accounting, Cost Control, and Cost Planning at Toyota

This chapter examines cost accounting and cost control as it relates to financial accounting, as well as cost planning at Toyota.

In February 1990, the author visited a Toyota accounting department and met with Goro Ito, section chief of the management department's cost management section; Hitoshi Washimi, chief of the management department's financial systems section; and Takashi Ishitera, chief engineer of the general department for production and planning. Mr. Ito and Mr. Washimi discussed cost accounting and cost control, while Mr. Ishitera answered questions regarding cost planning in the product planning and design stage.

Cost Accounting as a Goal of Financial Accounting. The type of cost accounting used at Toyota is process cost accounting. The individual parts of this process are arranged in order in Figure 2-1's representation of the company's manufacturing process.

Although general accounting uses standard cost accounting, at Toyota it is traditionally referred to as average cost. The average cost is established from individual material, parts, and products. Its value is determined twice a year for six-month periods. Interim receipts and partial payments relating to material, parts, and products, as well as monthly receipts and payments, are included in the average cost.

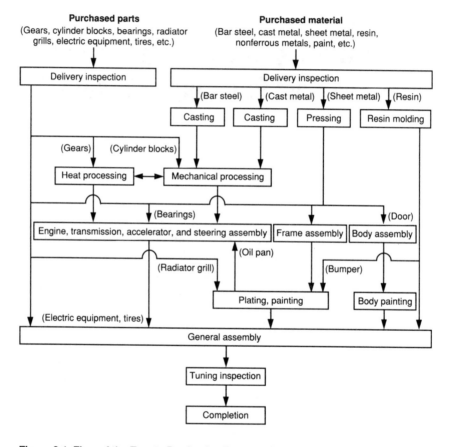

Figure 2-1. Flow of the Toyota Production Process

At the end of a period, an adjustment is made for the difference between the average cost and actual estimated cost. This lump sum adjustment is made in accordance with Japanese corporate income tax legislation, resulting in the product cost appearing first as a rough estimate and finally as a real cost estimate.

Item Cost Accounting. Cost by items of expenditure can be roughly divided into direct material costs and processing costs. At Toyota's settlement of accounts in June 1989, direct material costs as a percentage of the manufacturing cost were 85.5 percent. Of the direct material costs, 90 percent was spent on the purchase of parts. A similar cost ratio is typical for most Japanese auto makers.

Since direct cost accounting is not used, direct cost is not systematically divided into variable costs and fixed costs. However, variable costs are thought to be within the range of 85 to 90 percent. On the other hand, the division of costs into variable and fixed costs is done occasionally for a specific purpose. When this is the case, labor costs for actual work-site operations are paid as normal, fluctuating costs. Bonuses, pension payments, collection payments, and so forth are carried as fixed costs. In addition, depending on the purpose of the analysis, overtime compensation is carried under fluctuating costs. The profit-and-loss break-even point is rarely calculated. Instead, an estimate is made at the time of the settlement of accounts.

Advances in plant automation have influenced the cost structure considerably. With the development of automation, direct labor costs have gradually decreased. Nevertheless, the problem is that direct fixed costs (such as amortization costs for special equipment required for each type of car, maintenance costs, and insurance premiums) may be increasing. In view of this, although total direct labor costs did not fall significantly because of the complexity of production, types of cars that share specifications are now manufactured more efficiently by taking advantage of automation.

No special effort has been made to determine the percentage of direct labor target costs that have been achieved as a result of automation. While direct labor costs as a percentage of total manufacturing costs are likely to decrease, this percentage is not decreasing in periods of absolute total costs.

On the other hand, as the use of standardized equipment progresses, specialized equipment is no longer needed to produce a particular car model. The same equipment can often be used for various models at the same time. As a result, the direct fixed costs mentioned previously are now transferred to indirect fixed costs. Consequently, it could be said that direct fixed costs have been reduced.

This problem is emphasized by the fact that almost the entire line of Toyota automobiles consists of exclusive models. For instance, the Corona welding line usually welds only Corona automobiles (although the same line is sometimes used to weld both Corona and Carina automobiles). Establishing standard welding lines would mean increasing the effect of long-period investment by making it possible to run multiple car models through the line simultaneously.

Finally, operating costs (such as costs incurred in connection with advertising and commercials, compensation, and transportation) are calculated as a lump sum under financial accounting costs. Under special circumstances, however, operating costs are assessed for individual types of cars.

Process Cost Accounting. As explained, cost items can be divided into the two broad categories of material costs and processing costs (the latter includes individual processing costs). At Toyota, this is called general cost accounting calculated by individual groups. Cost accounting by group differs from the textbook definition of cost accounting, in which costs are classified by product type. At Toyota, individual groups at each plant are distinguished by job operations and organized in a specific order arrangement (department, section, division, group, team).

For example, besides an assembly department, the Toyota plant in this study has five departments: (1) an engineering department, (2) a quality control department, (3) a machinery department (a plant for the production of machinery), (4) a body department (a plant for the production of car bodies), and (5) a molding department (a plant for work with resins and molding). In the machinery department are several machinery sections, each with an assigned number. Thus, machinery section 2 processes and assembles differential carriers for rear-wheel operating devices in passenger cars. Within this section, there are several job operation divisions; job operation division 2 is composed of four groups of two teams. Figure 2-2 illustrates the organizational system of the Toyota workplace.

The plant organizes each unit under a department manager (or head), a section chief, a division manager, a group manager, and a team manager. Toyota's general cost accounting system, organized by groups according to job operations, is shown in Figure 2-2. Thus, the cost for each group is added to a total, while various types of parts are being produced within the same group. Consequently, Toyota's cost centers are divided into individual groups.

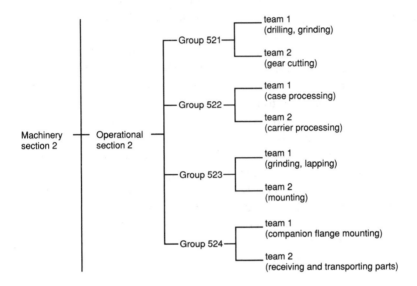

Figure 2-2. Organizational System at the Workplace

With ten plants, there are over 3,000 groups in the entire company. These cost centers, organized according to individual groups, are relatively small and no attempt is made to add the costs for each machine into a combined total. In this respect, cost accounting and cost control are organized symmetrically. For example, in the robot department of the body welding plant, a total of item costs is obtained for each machine. If there is a robot A and a robot B within one Toyota group, for example, they are lumped together as one group unit for the cost center's purposes.

Cost Accounting by Individual Products. The criterion for allocating the processing costs of individual processes to individual products is the number of labor hours. At Toyota, if the machines that produce all the parts are routed through a certain cost center, this is not considered an obstacle, even when the labor hour criterion is used. For instance, punch press machines differ according to their number of punches. Some workpieces pass through machine A alone, while others pass through both machine A and machine B.

Thus, a smaller cost center should be able to handle every machine for a number of parts. Likewise, if the cost center is expanded, certain parts will pass only through machine A while others will pass through all the machines. Since cost accounting is based on the labor hour standard, there should be no problem.

In contrast, it is difficult to estimate costs that are based on the number of hours put into new product development. For this reason, management estimates compensation costs that are based on machine-hours and labor costs that are based on labor hours.

The data about component parts required for the cost accounting criterion (standard cost accounting) are used in two forms: component parts tables for the purposes of production management (or MRP) and databases. Cost accounting of products, of secondary component parts, and of tertiary component parts is based on a cost criterion that is determined for each class of secondary and tertiary parts. These are included in a table of component parts in which each part belongs to a corresponding class classification.

Since there are many different types of parts, cost accounting by part is quite a nuisance and could not be conducted effectively without the use of computers. An example is the Toyota Corolla, which contains thousands of different types of parts. Because the company's database lists the components of each type of part, accounting is conducted for the product costs of thousands of products for the Corolla line only. (In this respect, Toyota differs from the prominent auto makers discussed in Chapter 8.)

Product profit and loss figures are routed to the sales department after the second period of settlement of accounts (in August and February) for administrative and control purposes. Although cost accounting by product is also done by financial accounting, its purpose is managerial accounting. Also, the difference in cost amounts is not broken down by individual products in order to clarify cost accounting by individual car models. Instead it is allocated by individual job operations in a lump sum that is applied to the sales cost.

Finally, job-specific cost accounting is also partially conducted. This is done, for instance, when an order for machine tools is received from a knock-down plant from abroad or when special orders are received.

Cost Control. *Budget Control in Toyota's Research and Development and Production Departments.* Cost accounting at Toyota starts from an improved target profit amount determining the difference between the target profit for the next period and the anticipated profit. Half of the amount is achieved by an increased sales volume; the remainder is realized by savings in expenditures.

Although improving the improved target profit amount is achieved mainly by eliminating fluctuating costs, savings are planned not only for the production departments. At Toyota, savings are also planned for the executive and research and development (R&D) departments. The same percentage of the improved amount, however, is not applied to the design and purchasing departments.

Improvements in all departments outside the plants are realized through budget control. Toyota's top management is authorized to set target savings within the framework of a budget for general operating costs. As far as the labor costs of clerks in the executive offices are concerned, overtime control is conducted by department within the framework of its personnel budget. For instance, let's say that overtime in this six-month period is to be limited to 20 hours per month per employee. Within the R&D department's budget for R&D costs, the plan stipulates reducing estimates for the next period over the present period. This represents direct material costs. In the sales department, the costs of outside orders for trial manufacturing are controlled by a budget for sales costs.

In the purchasing department, it is sometimes necessary to reduce the amount allotted for improvements, particularly during periods of recession brought on by oil shocks, yen appreciation, and similar factors. Achieving this reduction is one aim of price negotiations with outside vendors. On the other hand, during more stable periods, new purchases can be made without limiting the sum for improvements. Cost planning is based on prices planned for purchases that are linked to value engineering (VE). At the same time, an effort is made to secure purchases at lower prices. In other words, a significant reduction in the cost of purchased products is achieved over a long period of time.

Determining Cost Improvement Targets for the Company and Individual Plants. In terms of plant improvement, a target cost is first determined in the form of an overall cost improvement target for all the plants. This target cost is then divided up among the individual plants. The most important players in these cost meetings are the plant managers, department managers, and production managers. At the same time, managers responsible for product quality, production control, and accounting also participate. The accounting department represents top management.

The improvement targets allocated to each plant are earmarked for individual sections within each plant. Although the overall cost improvement target for the current period is determined during the cost meeting, a target reduction ratio is also sought for anticipated costs based on the criterion of real costs for the next period. The overall cost improvement target for all the plants (C) is determined by considering the following:

Real cost per car in current (A)

$$= \frac{\text{total real costs of previous period}}{\text{real number of cars in next period}}$$

Anticipated costs for all plants in current period (B)

$$= A \times \text{anticipated number of cars in next period}$$

Cost improvement target for all plants in current period (C)

$$= B \times \text{target reduction ratio per anticipated cost}$$

Although it is difficult to determine the target reduction ratio, it must be realized either with savings on expenditures through the profit improvement amount achieved during profit planning or by taking into account the real possibilities of reducing plant expenditures under existing conditions. Since the amount of cost improvement will form the balance of the target, its merit can be grasped easily by the plant workers. The total cost target has little meaning, however, because production is subject to such great fluctuations.

Each plant's cost quota (or percentage of the cost improvement target) is allotted based on the plant's size. The cost quota represents a plant's controllable costs. Controllable costs mean direct material costs, direct labor costs, variable indirect costs, and other costs not included under fixed costs, other reduction amortization costs, and similar costs.

The cost improvement target for the present period in all plants (C) is assigned to each plant as follows:

$$\text{Assigned cost ratio } (D) = \frac{\text{a plant's controllable costs}}{\text{controllable costs in all plants}}$$

$$\text{Total cost improvement in each plant } = C \times D$$

The distribution between plants is mutually agreed upon although it is often determined by an estimate of real results for the next period. Even if the accounting department already has a plan on the table, it is difficult to force this plan on the plant. Thus, a cost improvement target is assigned to each plant, and each plant is required to achieve this target. This sum is then allocated to and analyzed by each department, section, division, group, and team within the framework of a target control system, which will be described later.

The cost improvement target is determined by first presenting an estimated cost, which is subsequently reduced by some 10 percent. While this 10 percent reduction should equal the total standard cost, this is not always the case.

We cannot use the total standard cost as a tool of managerial control because it is influenced by factors other than those existing on the job site — such as fluctuating purchasing costs. In addition, even if the overall cost target is specified, it is difficult for people to remember. (On the other hand, knowing it is necessary to gain an understanding of the profitability of individual products.) Consequently, the target cost is not the same as the total standard cost. It is a reduced range of the cost or the actual amount of the cost improvements.

Improvements in Plant Labor Costs. We have determined that standard costs are revised twice a year for six-month periods. However, these standard costs are revised for subsequent periods in shorter time frames.

The number of workers in each group decreases from month to month by the number of sections in each plant. The performance time required to achieve results is also reduced. The scope of the decrease is measured every month based on achieved results. The standard cost, however, does not decrease every month because it is set for six-month periods.

To realize savings in labor costs in some plants, for example, it could be decided to reduce the total number of workers by 9 percent for a period of one year. This figure will be treated as a target worker reduction ratio of 9 percent. When the accounting department receives this figure, it will make an evaluation by also indicating in the cost the actual projected number of workers per month. In other words, the estimated real cost tends to decrease every month. It is then up to the plants to control the real number of workers. In this sense, the production control and accounting represent a dual form of control that serves to reduce labor costs.

To reduce labor costs, competitions are held between plants, sections, and groups to reduce the numbers of workers. The results are published in forecasts of performance labor costs based on the number of workers performing operations. These results are reflected in employee salaries, a strong incentive that is a unique feature of the Toyota group of companies.

When the standard number of workers is revised for the subsequent period, it does not necessarily follow that the number of workers performing operations is reduced. A final decision and revision is made only after the situation has been reviewed three times. This is based on elaborate rules that were determined originally by Taiichi Ohno, the person behind the Toyota production system.

(For the accounts of this manufacturing giant, see the following books by Taiichi Ohno published in English by Productivity Press: *Toyota Production System: Beyond Large-Scale Production* [1988], *Workplace Management* [1988], and *Just-In-Time for Today and Tomorrow* with Setsuo Mito [1988].)

Improvements in Material Savings. As explained, a double control is exercised over labor costs by the production control and accounting departments. Material costs of material, purchased parts, and supplementary materials (such as oil) are enforced independently by management in the workplace.

It was already noted that an improved cost figure is required from each plant with a target reduction ratio reflecting the estimated standard cost of the previous period. To achieve this target, each plant is assigned areas in which reduction is to be achieved in material and labor costs. As mentioned, efficiency is also displayed in the number of workers used in operations.

Improvements in material costs are judged by a standard that considers improvements in material waste. For instance, one objective in a punch press operation would be to reduce the waste of trim loss around the edges of the press plate during punching and cutting. Similar improvements are also sought in the processing of resins and in forging operations.

When an improvement total for costs of supplementary materials, tools, energy, and purchased parts is prepared, the accounting department will count and evaluate these improvements.

Since amortization costs are considered fixed costs, they are not entered as cost improvements under equipment improvement. This is one example illustrating how production control is not always in agreement with cost control.

The primary purpose of improving direct material costs is to enforce cost control at the plant level. The plan is designed to achieve lower planned costs for purchased parts and material costs. Nevertheless, a great deal of material is left over after the product has been finished. This is a result of the fact that more than ten thousand parts are needed to produce a single automobile. This is also why many value engineering (VE) proposals are brought forward by employees in the workplace — representing a valuable contribution.

It should also be noted that something similar to an analysis of variable costs appears in a textbook of target cost accounting; it seems to be designed for cost control at Toyota. In reality, this type of variance analysis is not often practiced at Toyota. One reason is that it is difficult to keep every receipt and payment slip required for such an analysis.

Target Control. Reducing the waste in labor and material costs was achieved by having the respective department, section, division, group, and team managers conduct target analysis at each organizational level of the plants. This type of target control is enforced on-the-spot down to the smallest business unit. Target control at Toyota is illustrated in Figures 2-3 and 2-4.

The Toyota Production System's Relationship to Accounting and Cost Control. Toyota's cost control system as explained so far provides only a general description of the Toyota method. The aim of the Toyota Production System is to reduce manufacturing costs by eliminating all factory waste. It is those methods that eliminate unnecessary workers and create a savings in labor costs. In this regard, the Toyota Production System is linked directly to the cost improvement target specified by the accounting department.

It is also known for achieving inventory reductions. Accordingly, at Toyota, reducing inventory is both the means and the result. Incidentally, even if inventory is reduced (for instance from $1 million to $500,000), this in itself will not be regarded by the accounting department as cost improvement. It would be inappropriate to say that inventory reduction programs are linked directly to cost controls stimulated by the accounting department.

Eliminating excess inventory can bring to light various problems in the plant. With reduced inventories, line stoppages can occur when products are out of stock due to an increased line speed. Line stoppages can also occur when goods of inferior quality are discovered. Exposing waste is important in preventing various types of line stoppages because it leads to vigorous efforts to eliminate waste. These types of indirect cost improvements are the main route to cost improvement in the Toyota Production System.

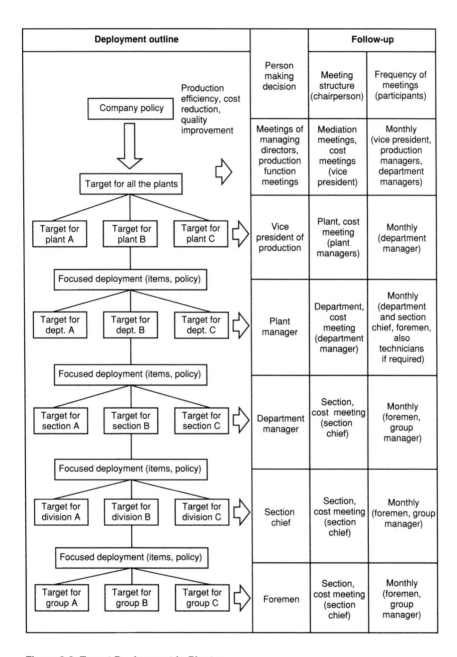

Figure 2-3. Target Deployment in Plants

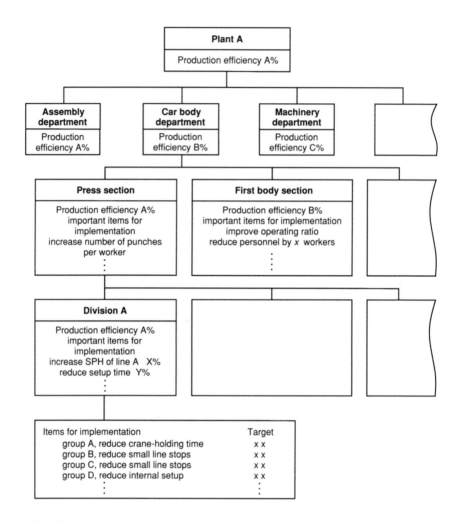

Figure 2-4. Concrete Deployment Patterns for Increased Production Efficiency

Cost Planning. The time frame for developing a new car in Japan — from planning, development, and design to sale of finished product — is four years. Although this may seem long, the market research conducted immediately after the line is discontinued is included in the four-year period. Specifically, the development period for a new car is approximately three years following the planning stage.

The development period is identical to the life cycle of a new car, which is again four years. According to the directives of Japan's

Ministry of International Trade and Industry (MITI), the model life of cars must not exceed four years. Although no cars have a model life as short as one or two months, those with the shortest life last only four years. The model life of trucks is four to ten years, with most averaging six to seven years.

Let's now consider how many items are required for a cost estimate in cost planning. This includes not only products manufactured in-house, but also parts purchased from outside vendors and an endless variety of nuts and bolts. More than 20,000 parts will be needed for the development of a new car, and parts such as nuts and bolts are not even included in the estimate of required items. As a result, it is necessary to conduct a new cost estimate for some 5,000 parts — those manufactured in-house and those supplied from outside.

To check whether or not the target cost is achieved after the car is assembled, the real estimated cost per car is calculated by comparing it to the target cost. While it is doubtful that it provides very useful information, this cost comparison is used to create the target cost of subsequent models.

The Cost Planning Process. Toyota's cost planning process is similar to that used by Daihatsu Industries and is described in Chapter 3. Toyota actually instructed Daihatsu in the creation of its system. An outline of the Toyota cost planning process is described in Figure 2-5.

Toyota's method differs in that Daihatsu's cost planning section oversees product development. Furthermore, the Daihatsu product managers who are responsible for inspecting the different car models are part of the technology planning department. They feel that close cooperation between sections is useful in cost planning from the standpoint of planning and new product design.

In contrast, the Toyota cost planning group belongs (1) to the cost control office of the accounting department and (2) to the cost planning office of the technology department. This arrangement makes it possible to apply Daihatsu's methods without major changes. At Toyota, data regarding estimates of the real costs of existing cars can be obtained easily from individual cost estimates at various design stages. Each method has advantages and disadvantages, making it difficult to declare one better than the other.

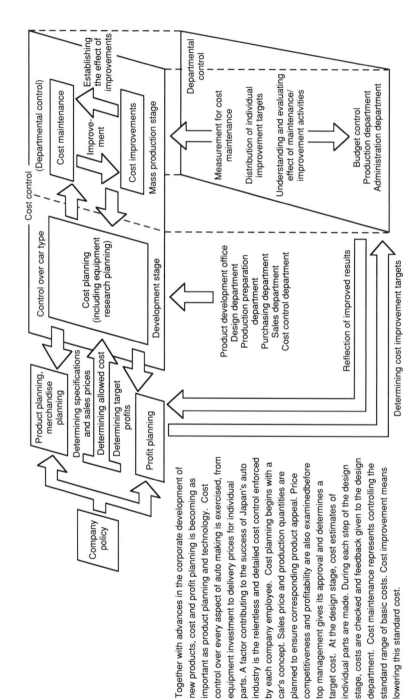

Together with advances in the corporate development of new products, cost and profit planning is becoming as important as product planning and technology. Cost control over every aspect of auto making is exercised, from equipment investment to delivery prices for individual parts. A factor contributing to the success of Japan's auto industry is the relentless and detailed cost control enforced by each company employee. Cost planning begins with a car's concept. Sales price and production quantities are planned to ensure corresponding product appeal. Price competitiveness and profitability are also examinedbefore top management gives its approval and determines a target cost. At the design stage, cost estimates of individual parts are made. During each step of the design stage, costs are checked and feedback given to the design department. Cost maintenance represents controlling the standard range of basic costs. Cost improvement means lowering this standard cost.

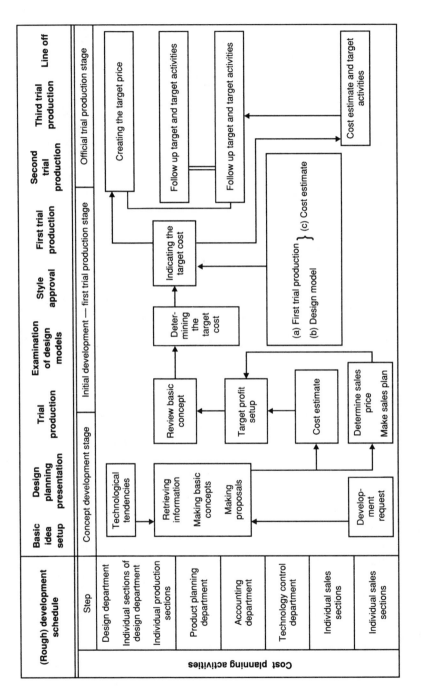

Figure 2-5. Toyota's Cost Planning Process

Compared to their counterparts in the Western auto industry, product managers in charge of new car development at Toyota (chief engineers) and at Daihatsu (chief inspectors of cars models) have broader responsibility and authority covering the range of development and design.

How is the target cost determined in Toyota's cost planning process? First, the target sales cost is determined by the sales department — not the chief engineer. The target sales cost is based on the sales figures of the competition.

Next, the target profit is calculated by the cost control office. It is determined from the correlation between the company's long-period profit ratio target and the present real profit ratio. In the case of new cars at Toyota, however, target profit per car is determined by top management during cost planning meetings.

Once the target profit is determined, a new product planning concept of the chief engineer is put forward as a proposal for a new car. The cost planning group subsequently considers the proposal in terms of its profit and loss elements. In this way, the profit of newly developed cars is evaluated. By comparing profit and loss to a tentative cost estimate based on the target sales cost, they determine whether or not the proposed car is capable of realizing the desired target profit.

The target profit is subtracted from the target sales price to determine the target cost. This target cost includes the cost development of every part manufactured in-house as well as the cost of every part ordered from outside vendors.

The target cost is then determined by the general control department for product planning and by the accounting department (representing the cost planning group of the cost control office). These departments exchange relevant information that is accessible to any employee. The current conditions determining the price are explained by the price planning group. This is necessary to ensure a relationship of mutual trust between the general control department for product planning and the accounting department. In particular, the estimated sales volume and the target sales price must be discussed at length with the sales department.

The most important new cars for development represent thousands of parts. That is why a representative base for part development is decided in consultation with the sales department. If the car in question is a sedan, a sedan base will be determined, while the development of types of parts applicable to other cars will be restricted. This representative base is designed in great detail by the general control department for product planning, and its highest cost is proposed during cost planning meetings. Thus, when the final sales price has been determined, it becomes possible to calculate the cost of several hundred cars.

Thus, the chief engineer (or product manager) is responsible for new car development and for achieving the target price in view of the target profit, and, as a result, for the profit and for the subsequent sales volume. Therefore, whether or not the new car will prove popular in the marketplace is a serious concern.

A question to ask about new car development is whether or not it is better to be more inclined toward sales or technology. Ideally, both are required equally. The success of Nissan's luxury car Cima is being attributed to the specialization of Nissan sales people as product managers. This sales sense is critical during new car development. On the other hand, once the design is clear, technology departments become more important. And again, once the Nissan model number is assigned, experienced sales personnel are indispensable for public relations work.

Calculating the Economic Efficiency of Investing in Equipment. At Toyota, calculating the economic efficiency of investing in equipment is the task of the production technology department — not of the accounting or product development departments. The recovery period of equipment is subtracted from the year's total costs (including interest) and compared to the amount that currently is proposed for new equipment. The resulting amount is then evaluated. Although the lifetime of equipment required for determining this recovery period varies, in the case of specialized machines it is usually three to four years. This corresponds to a car's life cycle that was discussed previously.

This method serves to reduce managerial costs by evaluating the efficiency of introducing new equipment without considering currency fluctuations over time. The evaluation represents a comparison of costs for accounting purposes only.

Other Items. The cost of individual products is presented to top management by the accounting department twice a year. Reports are prepared after the settlement of accounts in August and February. At this time, top management, the sales department, and the general control department for product planning receive the profit figures from new car models.

Since the sales department already knows the rolling stock prices, the accounting department does not have to send them a report regarding these prices. The actual determination of new car prices is left to the sales department, which drafts a proposal based on previously established standards. Prices are determined by taking into account any modifications made to the specifications of the new cars, such as the prices of competing car models. The task of top management is to come to a decision regarding this draft proposal.

Because the cost accounting department is located at company headquarters, there are no cost accountants in the individual Toyota plants. In this respect, the Toyota system differs significantly from the procedures used by most companies. At Nissan, for example, cost accountants are found in every plant. For this reason, a transfer cost is used between plants, creating a system of profit centers. Likewise, Hitachi employs a system of profit centers.

Regarding future trends at Toyota, I think it may be necessary to extend the awareness of what constitutes profit to every department of the company.

Remarks. All of Toyota's targets, from plantwide targets to targets for individual business units, are developed in great detail to avoid creating targets that are too general. As we can see in Figure 2-6's presentation of the flow of management throughout the production department, the production efficiency ratio (which serves as a yardstick for the evaluation of general productivity) is decided in mediation meetings. Cost improvements are subsequently determined in cost meetings.

Company officers who normally participate in mediation meetings include those working in production departments from the level of company vice president to the individual department managers. These meetings are occasions to exchange ideas emphasizing the importance of tasks in each workplace in addition to control cycles.

Target controls must be enforced in a way that guarantees sufficient flexibility of the determined targets and evaluations, as well as flexibility of respective programs and their implementation. When first determined, target controls are not formulated uniformly but are assigned in a manner compliant with conditions in each department. This is based on the principle that as much profit as possible

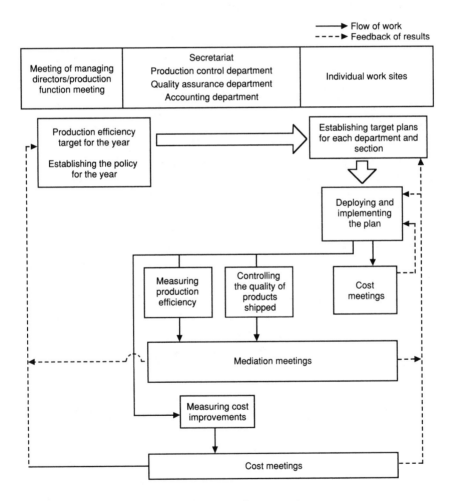

Figure 2-6. Managing the Overall Production Department

should be realized when and where it is best for this profit to be realized. Finally, even though each department will set up a different strategy to achieve the targets, the important thing is that the targets be achieved throughout the organization.

As far as evaluation is concerned, this is not a simple evaluation of production efficiency alone. It is also an evaluation of production conditions, product quality, cost, and other factors evaluated during a model change, for instance. The evaluation is modified from the moment the model comes off-line to correspond to the number of elapsed months.

Other problems cannot be solved within a limited structure. Projects that concern the company as a whole have been initiated to deal with such problems. These projects determine important management topics and processes. They can be formulated at any time by drawing upon innovative activities such as brainstorming in committee meetings on cost improvement or product quality.

Another important activity for the structure of plant units revolves around plant autonomy research circles. All members of plant managerial committees belong to this circle. Its activities serve to eliminate bottlenecks in the plant and to promote cost improvements and increased efficiency. This activity is being developed by the Toyota group of companies. Currently, thirty-four companies participate in a car manufacturing autonomy research circle that emphasizes parts and car assembly. Thirty companies have joined a distribution autonomy research circle that emphasizes distribution. The purpose of another movement is to develop improvements across the overall organizational structure. These are introduced during the aforementioned mediation meetings.

A topic common to all of these activities is planning the transfer of targets or shifting their emphasis. This is seen in Figure 2-7. The temporary and local shifts in production efficiency through production assignments involve eight companies responsible for assembly, the introduction of universally used equipment, the transfer and distribution of personnel, and so on. These shifts, when properly applied, represent a real contribution to maintaining and improving Toyota's overall productivity.

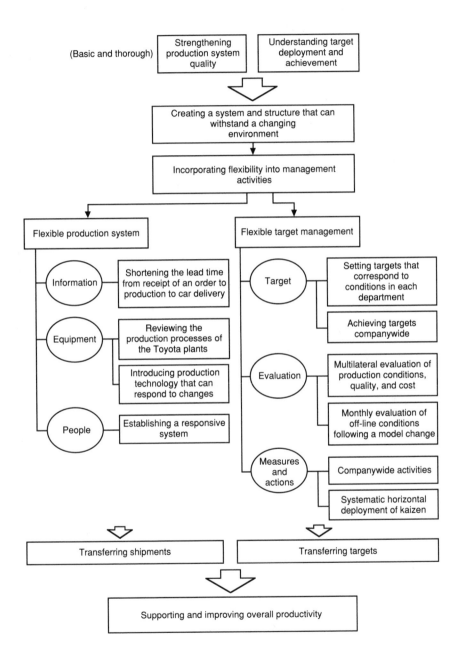

Figure 2-7. Incorporating Flexibility into Management Activities

3

Total Cost Management System in Japanese Automobile Corporations*

The Japanese auto industry has expanded and earned large profits consistent with Japan's high economic growth. Due to the lower economic growth and import restrictions of the United States and other nations, however, the auto industry is now in a position — even in Japan — where it cannot avoid a decrease in its growth rate. Companies experiencing the greatest difficulty with growth need to implement cost reduction measures to increase profits. These measures include eliminating waste and producing high quality goods at the lowest possible price. Cost reduction methods have a natural association with total cost management, which is largely concerned with product planning and design activities.

To follow the steps of total cost management, a corporation must:

1. plan a product that meets the customer's demand for quality,

---

* Reprinted with permission from *Applying Just-In-Time: The American/Japanese Experience*, Y. Monden, ed., (Atlanta: Institute of Industrial Engineers, 1986). This chapter is a revised version of an article co-authored with Yoshiteru Noboru.

2. determine a target cost under which the customer's demand for quality is attainable by using a blueprint based on value engineering (cost reduction in a narrower sense), and
3. determine which processes achieve the target cost in production performance (cost control).[1]

Nearly every company in the Toyota Group has completely implemented the total cost management system under the guidance of Toyota Motors. Toyota considers the system capable of horizontally governing the cost management of multiple departments. The total cost management system is of great significance in what Toyota calls "functional management."[2]

The total cost management system discussed in this chapter takes a similar approach. A characteristic of the system is that accounting takes on a more subservient role when compared to management science. Many Japanese manufacturers have implemented this approach and broken down their cost management departments as follows:

- *cost control section:* profit planning, budget control, cost accounting for financial accounting
- *cost planning section:* general advocate of cost planning, cost estimation by blueprints, cost reduction by value engineering (VE)
- *cost improvement section:* general promotion of cost improvement activities at the factory

The cost management department supervises the general progress of the total cost management processes mentioned above. Many other departments, however, also play a definitive role in the process. These include the corporate planning, product planning, exporting, technology planning, design, purchasing, and production technology departments. As a result, the relative significance of conventional accounting or cost control decreases. From a profit standpoint, a focus on cost as an economic measure of value unites the entire corporation under the coordination of cost management in creating innovative approaches to cost reduction and cost control.

A cost management system is generally divided into these three stages:

1. corporate planning
2. cost planning
3. cost improvement

First, an outline of the three stages is explained. At the corporate planning stage, a long-term corporate profit plan is established. The target profit of each product and the required capital outlay and human resources are presented in a structural project plan. A target profit is identified for each new product development planning project. Eventually, the target profit will be one of the objectives to be accomplished through cost planning activities.

The cost planning stage is the point when cost management is divided into cost reduction and cost control. Broadly speaking, the corporate management planning of stage 1 is included in the cost planning of stage 2. A simple interpretation of cost planning would be two processes roughly classified as: (1) the process of planning a specific product that satisfies customer needs and takes on a target cost inferred from the target profit of the new product, and (2) the design department's process for monitoring the accomplishment of the target cost using VE and a comparison to established cost estimates.

Finally, to be more accurate, the final cost improvement stage can be restated as the cost maintenance and cost improvement stage. This step controls the target cost for the blueprint. The blueprint identifies the actual production processes determined at the cost planning stage. Cost improvement activities continue to be conducted throughout a car model's life.

These processes are shown in Figure 3-1. The following discussion will refer to this figure.

Corporate Planning. For Japanese companies, the corporate planning stage is when a medium-term (three- or four-year period) profit plan for the whole corporation is established. The medium-term profit plan is established anticipating both variable and period costs. Its purpose is to (1) establish a target profit for each period and (2) lower the company's break-even point. It is well known that the break-even sales point is obtained by dividing fixed costs by the contribution margin ratio. Therefore, to improve the contribution margin three years down

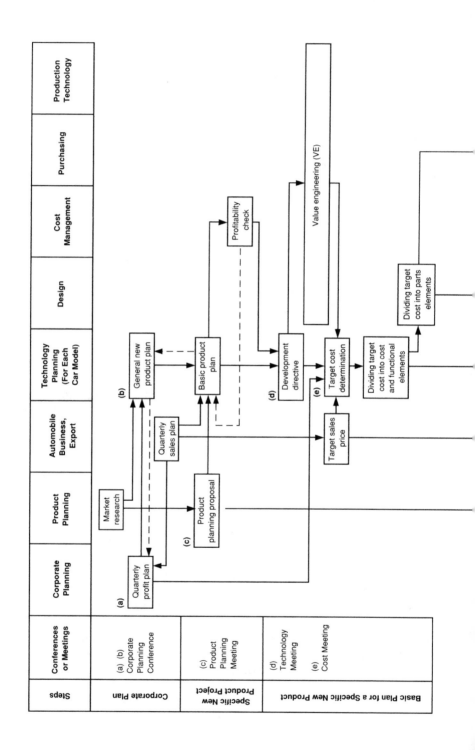

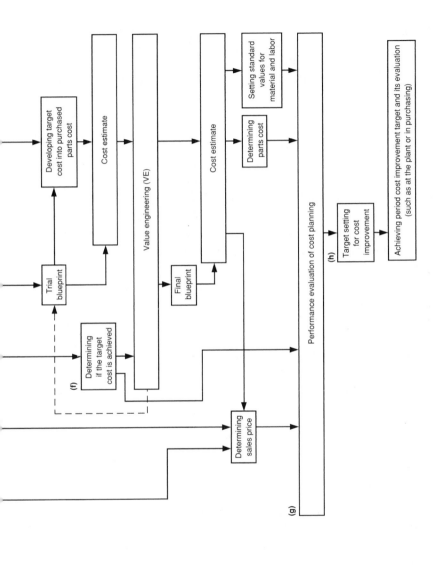

Figure 3-1. System for Cost Planning

the line, the question becomes: what new approach will be taken for the new product development plan and the sales plan of each automobile model during project planning? Reducing fixed costs is addressed in the medium-term profit plan. Fixed costs can be adjusted through project planning to include equipment investment, personnel, and funds procurement. Through this planning process, the target profit of each new product is determined.

The medium-term corporate plan is determined at top management's corporate planning meeting and is drafted by the corporate planning department responsible for the company's overall planning activities. Among the project plans that comprise management's corporate plan are new product development plans. These plans are drafted by the technology planning department and are revised in the process of establishing a corporate new product plan. In the corporate new product plan, the chairpersons (or departmental managers supervising each automobile model) identify the life cycle of each model by year, draft any model changes or modifications, and integrate them into new product groups. When a corporate new product plan is authorized at a corporate planning meeting, it is presented in the form shown in Figure 3-2.

Cost Planning. We now proceed to the four-step cost planning stage:

   1. specific new product project
   2. basic plan for a specific new product
   3. product design
   4. production transfer plan

Step 1 occurs when management formulates its recommendations for new products with new car development, model changes, and modifications. The basic plan for a specific new product will establish the target cost necessary to achieve the required target profit for new products. During product design, cost is estimated based on a design blueprint and VE discussions. Processes are redesigned where there is a gap between target cost and the estimate. Finally, the production transfer plan, which sets the target cost for the production stage, is prepared. Production equipment requirements, the cost of parts, raw material standards, labor hours, and sales price are all determined at this stage.

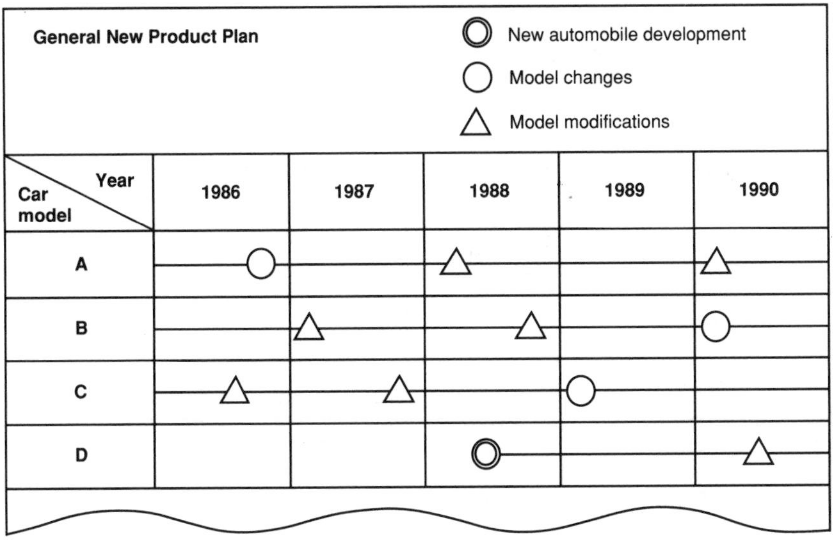

General New Product Plan					
○ New automobile development					
○ Model changes					
△ Model modifications					
Car model \ Year	1986	1987	1988	1989	1990
A	○		△		△
B		△	△		○
C	△	△	○		
D			◎		△

Figure 3-2. Corporate New Product Plan

Specific New Product Project. At the first stage of a specific new product project, product planning asks technology planning to determine the type of new product to be developed based on market research. After observing the marketplace, the technology planning department determines the objective and content of the model changes required to meet user trends. The product planning proposal is usually presented at a top management product planning meeting. Figure 3-3 illustrates a draft for a specific product project.

Under the supervision of the technology planning product manager, the project progresses to the planning stage to establish the basic product plan. The basic structure consisting of those items critical to cost behavior are determined during this step. For example, engine type, drive type (front engine, front drive or front engine, rear drive), body size, setting of performance targets, components

Product Planning Proposal	Preparation date
	Product planning department
1 Background	2 Aim
3 Contents	4 Full grades of this car model
5 Sales price & expected sales quantity	6 Sales starting date

Figure 3-3. Product Planning Proposal

for new development, and the determination whether or not existing parts will be improved are established in the planning stage.

It can be said that the approximate cost of a new product such as a car model is largely determined by the basic product plan. Therefore, the cost management department examines whether or not the plan can provide the target profit. They collect information on the product manager's recommendations about the product structure and estimate the cost of the planned car based on existing products. In addition, the payback period of invested capital is reviewed in conjunction with sales projections. As a result of this profitability check, the cost management department may request modifications to the basic plan when the project does not appear profitable.

The Basic Plan for a Specific New Product. After reviewing feedback several times and following the profitability check, a top management technology team determines whether or not to continue project development. Information for each department involved in the development is disseminated in the form of a directive that generally includes:

- development target
- basic development plan
- basic policies
- structural outline
- quality target
- conditions for production
- cost planning
- weight target
- development schedule

This is the beginning of the basic plan for a specific new product. The purpose of the basic plan is to determine the major cost factors, such as design and structure. It is also the step when target costs are assigned to the appropriate departments. It is appropriate to say that the success of cost planning depends on the extent to which cost reduction is achieved in this stage, the main activities of which are explained in the following discussion.

Cost reduction through VE activities. In the technology planning department, the product manager of the car model in question holds a meeting to explain the basic plan communicated in the development directive and to elicit each department's cooperation. At this point, a thorough VE analysis is required to identify innovative yet cost effective product features that will fulfill customer demands. The focus should be on material requirements and the details of the manufacturing process.

Each section of the design department develops a detailed structural plan, after dividing the product's basic plan into the component parts for which they have responsibility. At the same time, they identify cost reduction strategies, such as a new processing system or a new material. The production technology department is responsible for generating a VE proposal that addresses improvement at the factory level. This includes manufacturing production equipment. In the factory, the cost reduction activities of existing products are reviewed and improvement proposals related to new or altered products are generated. To provide adequate communication of the various VE proposals, several discussion meetings are held by the departments supervising the various aspects of product development. Discussions may be held, for example, about the clay model of the planned car or a disassembled car of a competitor. Each proposal is subjected to a technological and profitability screening. As a result, problems worthy of further consideration are separately identified.

Establishing the target cost. Using the basic plan communicated through the development directives, target sales prices are gathered from the appropriate business divisions, in this example, the domestic and export auto divisions. The target cost is approximated by subtracting the target or required profit established in the medium-term corporate plan from the sales price. The result is the allowable cost.

Simultaneously, the cumulative cost estimate of the product's basic plan, after adjusting for the financial effect of VE proposals (or the potential cost) is calculated. There is usually a gap between the allowable and potential costs, which is closed after allocation of fixed costs. As a result of this allocation process, a formal target cost of a representative automobile is determined and subsequently authorized at a top management cost meeting. At this point, the probability of achieving the target gross profit of the product in question is estimated by examining the target contribution margin per unit, the target sales units, and the target equipment investment. From management's viewpoint, it is best to plan for the greatest possible target profit because the initial allowable cost is likely to be high. The potential cost accumulated from a financial interpretation of present conditions, however, is not an appropriate cost objective. It is necessary to establish a target cost that represents an attainable objective and is both economical and motivational.

Developing the cost and functional elements of the target cost. The technology planning department first develops the total target cost (for example, of a single car) by identifying cost and functional elements with the help of the cost management department. Identifying the cost elements requires separating the target cost into material, parts, direct labor, special equipment (such as stamping dies or welding machines), depreciation, overhead, direct sales, administration, and so forth. The cost elements of the existing products are used as a basis for this breakdown. When planning a product, the basic structure (including internal and external manufacturing) is considered although not yet finalized.

Developing the functional elements classifies the target cost into structural categories, similar to the way in which sections in the design department are classified, such as the engine, transmission system, and chassis. In this process, the product manager's recommendations for the product plan are presented according to each function's cost. Comparing these costs to the current product's itemized costs should determine the relative emphasis for each function, as shown in Figure 3-4. This information is passed on to the design department.

Cost Elements / Functions	Material Costs	Purchased Parts Costs	Direct Labor Costs	. . . . .	Total
Engine	$	$	$		$
Transmission System					
Chassis					
⋮					
Total *					

* The amount should be presented either in the form of the total cost of a single car (in the case of new model or model change) or as a deviation from the existing car (in the case of model modifications).

Figure 3-4. Target Cost Broken into Cost Elements and Functions

Developing part elements of the target cost. The design department develops the target cost for each part as directed by the technology planning department. Each section of the design department

Function		Assembly Number				Name						
Major Units	Parts Number	Parts Name	Quantity	Process	Car Model			Materials Cost	Purchased Parts Cost	Direct Labor Cost		
					A	B	C			Department	Worker Hours (Minimum)	Amount
									$	$		$

Figure 3-5. Target Cost Broken into Part Elements

separates its functions into major units (such as front accelerator and front and rear brakes), and then further subdivides them, since a car's target cost includes a number of purchased and internally produced parts. At this stage, the design department elaborates on the product manager's recommendations for the function and structure of the automobile relative to parts. At the same time, the VE proposals prepared in step 1 are considered and the design department begins to focus on the cost reduction objective. This situation is summarized in Figure 3-5.

Product Design. Next, the design department drafts a trial blueprint that must show the given target cost of each part while meeting quality standards. This provides for the incorporation of cost into the blueprint. Needless to say, experienced designers are required for this task, and each department involved in product development must cooperate by supplying information and assistance.

The target cost and the trial blueprint are presented to outside vendors, who account for 60 to 70 percent of the cost. The vendors present VE proposals using their own specialized techniques and expertise.

Based on this first trial blueprint, a trial product is manufactured. At the same time, a cost estimate is prepared. The production technology department supplies information about the cost of external parts to the cost management department, which incorporates this information with figures on parts produced in-house. The possibility of achieving the target cost is examined based on the accumulation of this information. Each department cooperates in performing additional VE activities if target cost expectations are not met. The results of these additional activities are returned to the design department and the appropriate adjustments are made to the trial blueprint. After repeating this process several times, the final blueprint is drafted. This step accomplishes two goals: (1) it ensures that sections in charge of certain parts have accomplished the target cost based on the trial blueprint cost estimate and (2) it promotes VE activities.

Production Transfer Plan. The production transfer plan is the last step in cost planning. After repeating the circular process (trial blueprint, cost estimate, VE activities, adjustments to the trial blueprint), the final blueprint is drawn. Internal capital equipment requirements are finalized and external production equipment is prepared with the appropriate vendors. Based on the final blueprint and completion of production equipment installation, a final cost estimate is prepared. It is now six or seven months prior to the start of production. The cost management department reviews the final cost estimate and presents it to the business department as a reference for establishing the sales price for domestic and foreign markets. Based on the final estimate and testing results, the production technology department establishes standard values for the material required for each part's coating requirements, labor hours, and so on. These standard values are immediately presented to the factory. Using the final estimated sales price, the purchasing department starts negotiating with vendors for parts prices. In principle, the sales price is determined by the time production begins.

After accomplishing these final tasks, the planning stage of cost planning is complete. The planning stage continues in the production and sales departments, where performance is measured and evaluated. In this case, the performance in question occurs three months after production has started because a greater number of labor hours and abnormalities are inflated as a result of the learning curve during the first three months of production. Normal production values are commonly achieved by the end of the fourth month.

To compare the target and actual costs of purchased parts requires a comparison of the target price of a part and the actual purchase price. The direct labor cost, however, is not compared from a dollar perspective. Since the target was determined by the number of labor hours, target and actual labor hours are compared.

There are two purposes for evaluating cost planning's performance. One reason is to ascertain whether or not the target cost established in the basic new product plan is being achieved. If not, it clarifies who is responsible — the blueprint (design) or the production process (purchasing/factory). The second reason is to judge whether or not the cost planning activities were effective. The following questions are addressed: Did activities proceed according to the development schedule? Were production methods satisfactory?

Were cost planning activities useful? The results of this evaluation are used in subsequent product planning cycles.

This performance evaluation is based on a comparison between target and actual costs. Japanese companies regard this comparison strictly as a control over cost planning and as the final step of the cost planning process. In this respect, it is necessary to differentiate daily cost control activities between target and actual costs in attempting to achieve the target cost.

Cost Improvement Activities. As previously mentioned, a final evaluation of cost planning is made following the third month of production. If the target cost is missed by a large margin, an improvement team is organized to conduct a thorough value analysis (VA). To distinguish our terms, value engineering (VE) refers to cost improvements that address basic functional changes in the new product development stage. Value analysis refers to cost improvements that require design changes.

The target cost should be firmly established during the planning stage. Any increases subsequent to cost reduction losses after production must be minimized. There are instances, however, when production commences prior to completion of the target cost as a result of delays in the development schedule or planning changes.

Cost Improvement Committee. When failure to achieve the target cost occurs, a special project team called "the X-model cost improvement committee" is organized. In most cases, the committee is comprised of the person in charge of cost control as the chairperson, the product manager as co-chairperson, and the cost control department as committee members. With managers in charge, the committee then breaks into two subcommittees — one focusing on purchased parts and one focusing on the individual processing costs of each department involved with the product in question. These subcommittees conduct intense VE activity and usually last for six months.

VA activities always include the following processes: drafting the blueprint, trial production, experiment, and evaluation. Considerable effort from each participating department is necessary for the success of these activities. The establishment of a cost improvement committee implies that a car model's improvement is a top priority. Keeping the process — from drafting the blueprint to evaluation — as short as possible minimizes lost opportunities.

Periodic Cost Improvement. Periodic cost improvement means reaching a cost reduction target established for every field as a result of a short-term profit plan. Cost items are divided into two groups: (1) variable cost items (such as purchased parts and factory variable overhead) and (2) fixed cost items (such as indirect labor costs and overhead expenses).

Variable overhead. Reducing purchased parts cost is achieved through VA and price negotiation. Periodically, VA sets forth the total amount and target total amount of cost reduction expected from each product. VA proposals are received from all departments and vendors. Every process from subsequent investigation to part changes is managed within the system. Proposals from outside vendors are encouraged; they are pushed through the resolution system and rewarded based on the results. The purchasing department begins price negotiations with vendors to reduce costs during the periodic price reform stages. To avoid an exclusive focus on price reductions, guidance for parts improvement is given to the factories involved.

The variable costs of a factory (such as material, coating, indirect material, energy, and direct labor costs) are managed by setting a cost reduction target for each product type. The purchasing department supervises the purchased cost management from outside suppliers, such as material and coating costs. The factories primarily work on reducing consumption through VA and savings. Direct labor costs are quantified in labor hours. At the beginning of each period, the target for reduced direct labor cost is determined for each factory and automobile type. Monthly targets are set for each work area and given to supervisors.

Management of the variable cost items already mentioned can be called variable (or flexible) budget management when the target cost per unit is previously determined.

Fixed costs. Fixed costs are also analyzed by applying the total cost reduction target. Once the labor costs of general management and related departments are identified, a target incorporating the number of personnel, overtime hours, and an appropriation of expenses is established. These are under management's budgetary control. The total amount of these cost items is compiled from each individual structural plan in the overall management plan. The individual structural plan includes sales, personnel, and equipment investment plans. Fixed costs are allocated by cost category and by factory within the total budget plan.

Management by Objectives and the Cost Accounting System. In comparing the target and actual costs during cost maintenance improvement activities, accountants are likely to recall the traditional cost control system. As discussed earlier, cost control activities are not based on the conventional standard costing system. They are based either on quantity units (such as labor hour management or management by *kanban*) outside the standard costing system, or they are conducted departmentally by subjecting each cost item to the budgetary management process. Some Japanese automobile companies use the standard cost system. At present, however, the main purpose of a standard cost system is considered to be budget accounting.

The reason cost control (or cost improvement) is conducted outside the standard cost system is not because of a lack of importance, but rather because of a degree of importance warranting an independent system.[3] Since standard costs have constraints from a financial accounting perspective, they are inappropriate measures for management. A typical constraint is the infrequency with which quantity standards (such as processing time per product unit or material requirements) are revised. Normally, these standards are maintained at the same level throughout the year.

The Japanese auto industry, therefore, differentiates between standard cost and target cost, controlling production by the target cost. In the current standard costing system of a certain Japanese company, for example, the standard processing hours per part (or product) for each cost division are determined first. By multiplying the standard hours by the processing cost allocation rate, the standard processing cost per part (or product) is determined. The standard processing hours by division are the expected numerical value and are averaged as the yearly mean. Therefore, the same value is used throughout the year. The target value of a given month varies, however, and is derived by multiplying cycle time by the number of labor hours. The value decreases a little every month because of what the Toyota production system calls "manufacturing process improvement." Cycle time in this context is the required production time per part or per product (for one process), and usually is quite short (maybe one or two minutes). Multiplying the labor hours by the cycle time becomes the standard production time per product unit. The target labor time is derived from the target reduction rate anticipated in the profit plan. Labor time calculated this way is the evaluation measure. The monthly reduction target is fixed during a given period.

In a month when large quantities of products are expected, measures must be taken to increase overtime or shorten cycle time to provide the necessary increases in direct labor time. Increasing direct labor time, however, is generally discouraged. Instead, each work area is encouraged to improve the manufacturing process. Allocating individual worker targets, in accordance with scheduled production levels, should emphasize process improvement in attempting to achieve the target production. This is what the Toyota production system calls "worker savings."[4] In contrast, it must be made clear that the standard accounting time should be the same throughout the year — not changed to accommodate monthly targets.

Conclusion. Cost reduction activities have been conducted with primary emphasis on cost maintenance and improvement. It has long been recognized that the application of management by objectives (MBO) at the product development stage is important in achieving increased profit margins. Under this method, target profits are achieved by establishing a new product's target profit in accordance with the company's long-term profit plan. This requires calculating the target cost, based on the target profit and VE activities applied at the developmental and planning stages. Accordingly, each company in Japan integrates a product's characteristics, its method of development, and the skills of its supervisory employees in creating production systems.

Nevertheless, several problems exist at present. For example, the new product development department has too much work. The cost planning steps as presented here assume a three-year lead in scheduling new product development, with heavy emphasis on the first year. To meet the demands of new users, increased diversification, competition, and technological advancement, the development department is forced to work simultaneously on several models and shorten development periods. As a result, business efficiency becomes increasingly important to cost planning activities that are supposed to receive appropriate labor resources.

Recently developed computer-aided design (CAD) and computer-aided manufacturing (CAM) systems are becoming indispensable for auto makers. CAD computerizes the requisite data for design, enabling design work to be done on a graphic display. The computer — not the worker — quickly and precisely carries out data processing and complicated curved lines or three-dimensional designs. CAM produces tapes for numerical control (NC) production machines that produce parts according to the data in the CAD-drawn blueprint. Although futuristic, there is an attempt being made to combine CAD/CAM into a robot or flexible manufacturing system (FMS).

To solve the problem just mentioned, cost estimation requires improvement. The ability to estimate the product manager's recommendation from an outline before the blueprint is drawn and the ability to promptly estimate the cost during and after blueprint completion are two key factors in accomplishing the ultimate target.

In conventional cost estimating, the engineering department designs the process plan based on a blueprint and estimates the value of factors such as material consumption and processing time. The cost management department multiplies the unit cost of material and the processing cost rate by the material consumption and processing time, respectively. Although an estimate of the cost planning activity for each part is often documented on the blueprint, not all cost estimating systems (for example, conventional cost systems) work that way. Cost estimating during blueprint preparation requires instant judgment, and the data needed does not have to be sent to a supervising department. The designers themselves must be able to judge

4

Framework of the Just-In-Time Production System*

The Toyota production system developed and promoted by Toyota Motors is being adopted by many Japanese companies in the aftermath of the 1973 oil crisis. Although the main purpose of the system is to reduce costs, it also helps increase the turnover ratio of capital (total sales/total assets) and improve the total productivity of a company.

Even during periods of slow growth, the Toyota production system could make a profit by decreasing costs in a unique manner — that is, by completely eliminating excessive inventory or workforce. We would probably not overstate our case by saying that this is another revolutionary production management system. It follows the Taylor system (scientific management) and the Ford system (mass-assembly line). This chapter examines the basic idea behind this production system, how it makes products, and the specific areas in which Japanese innovation can be seen. The framework of this production system is examined as a unit by connecting its basic ideas or goals with the various tools and methods used for achieving these goals.

---

* Reprinted with permission from *Toyota Production System*, Yasuhiro Monden (Atlanta: Institute of Industrial Engineers, 1983).

Basic Idea and Framework. The Toyota production system is a reasonable method of making products because it completely eliminates unnecessary production elements to reduce costs. The basic idea in such a production system is to produce the kind of units needed, at the time needed, in the quantities needed. The realization of this concept would eliminate unnecessary intermediate and finished product inventories.

Even though the system's most important goal is cost reduction, three subgoals must be achieved before its primary objective is achieved.

1. *Quantity control* enables the system to adapt to daily and monthly demand fluctuations in quantity and variety.
2. *Quality assurance* ensures that each process will supply only defect-free units to subsequent processes.
3. *Respect for the worker* must be cultivated to allow full use of the human resources necessary for attaining the system's cost objectives.

It should be emphasized that these three goals cannot exist or be achieved independently. They influence each other and the primary goal of cost reduction. A special feature of the Toyota production system is that the primary goal cannot be achieved without realizing these subgoals, and vice versa. All goals are outputs of the same system. With productivity as the ultimate purpose and guiding concept, the Toyota production system strives to realize each of the goals for which it was designed.

Before discussing the Toyota production system in detail, an overview, which is shown in Figure 4-1, is in order. The outputs or results side (costs, quality, and labor) as well as the inputs or constituents side of the Toyota production system are depicted.

A continuous flow of production, or adapting to demand changes in quantity and variety, is created by achieving two key concepts: just-in-time (JIT) and autonomation, the two pillars of the Toyota production system. "Just-in-time" means producing the needed units in the needed quantities at the needed time. "Autonomation" *(jidoka)* may be loosely interpreted as autonomous defect control. It supports JIT by never allowing defective units from a preceding process to flow into and disrupt a subsequent process. Two concepts also important to the Toyota production system include "flexible workforce" *(shojinka)*, which means varying the number of workers based on demand changes, and "creative thinking or inventive ideas" *(soikufu)*, capitalizing on worker suggestions.

To implement these four concepts, Toyota has established the following systems and methods:

1. The *kanban* system maintains JIT production.
2. A production-leveling method allows adaptation-to-demand changes.
3. Shortened setup times reduce production lead times.
4. Standardizing operations achieves line balancing.
5. Improved machine layouts promote multi-skilled workers and the flexible workforce concept.
6. Small group improvement activities and a worker suggestion system reduce the workforce and increase morale, respectively.
7. A visual control system achieves autonomation.
8. A "functional management" system promotes companywide quality control.

Just-In-Time Production. The idea of producing what is needed in the needed quantities at the needed time is described by the words "just-in-time." Just-in-time means, for example, that in the process of assembling the parts needed to build a car, the subassemblies needed by the subsequent processes should arrive at the production line exactly when needed and in the quantity needed. To realize JIT companywide, unnecessary inventories as well as storage areas and warehouses in the plant will be completely eliminated. Inventory-carrying costs will be diminished and the ratio of capital turnover will increase.

To rely solely on the central planning approach (informing all processes simultaneously of the production schedules) makes it difficult to achieve just-in-time in all processes for a product like an automobile, which consists of thousands of parts. In the Toyota system, therefore, it is necessary to look at the production flow conversely; in other words, a subsequent process goes to the preceding

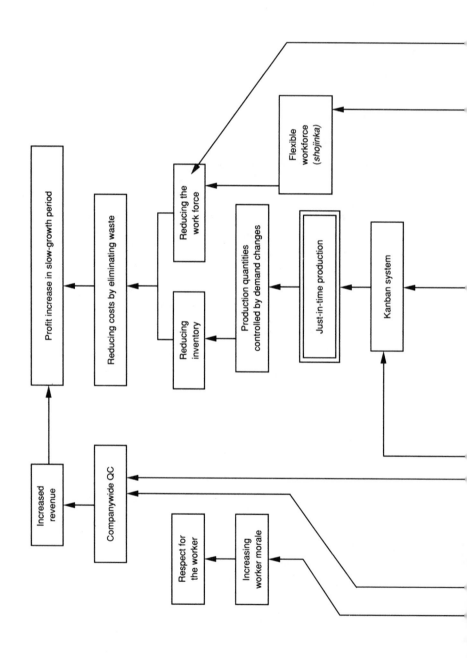

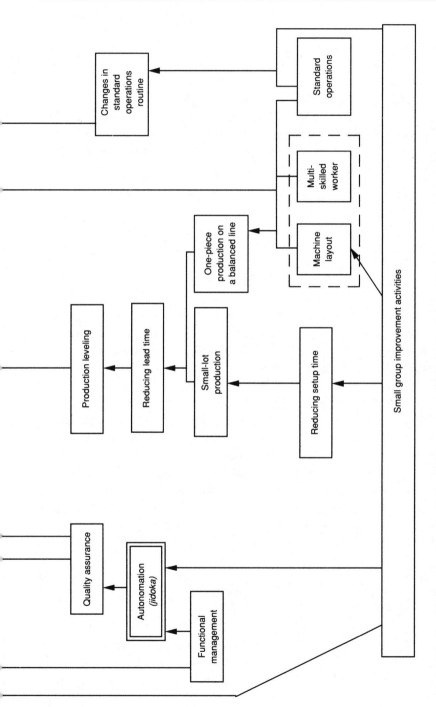

Figure 4-1. How Costs, Quantity, Quality, and Respect for the Worker Are Improved by the Toyota Production System

process to withdraw the needed units in the needed quantities when needed. The preceding process then produces the number of units withdrawn.

In this system, the type and quantity of units needed are written on a tag card called a *kanban*. Kanban are sent to a preceding process from the subsequent process. This results in better communication between processes as well as better quantity control. Toyota's kanban system is supported by the following:

- production leveling
- job standardization
- reducing setup time
- improvement activities
- improved machine layout
- autonomation

Kanban System. Many people call the Toyota production system a kanban system. This is incorrect. The Toyota production system is a way to make products, whereas the kanban system is a way to manage JIT production methods. In short, the kanban system is an information system to control the production quantities in and between processes. Unless the various prerequisites of this system are implemented perfectly (process design, standardized operations, production leveling, and so on), just-in-time will be achieved with difficulty, even with the introduction of the kanban system.

A kanban is usually a card put in a rectangular vinyl envelope. The two principle kinds used are withdrawal and production-ordering kanban. A "withdrawal kanban" tells the subsequent process to withdraw a certain quantity, while a "production-ordering kanban" tells the preceding process what quantity to produce. These cards circulate within Toyota plants, between Toyota and its many cooperative companies, and within the plants of cooperative companies. In this way, kanban contribute information on withdrawal and production quantities to achieve JIT production.

Suppose we are making products *A*, *B*, and *C* on an assembly line. The parts necessary to produce these products are *a* and *b*, which are produced by the preceding machining line (see Figure 4-2). Parts *a* and *b* produced by the machining line are stored behind it, and the line's production-ordering kanban are attached to these parts. The transporter from the assembly line making product *A* will go to the machining line to withdraw the needed part *a* with its withdrawal kanban. Then, at storage *a*, he picks up as many boxes of this part as his withdrawal kanban dictates and detaches the production-ordering kanban attached to these boxes. He returns again to the assembly line with both the boxes and the withdrawal kanban.

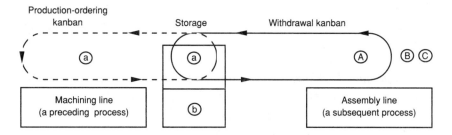

Figure 4-2. The Flow of Two Types of Kanban

At this time, the production-ordering kanban showing the number of units withdrawn are left at the machining line's storage *a*. These kanban will be the dispatch information to the machining line. Part *a* is then produced in the quantity directed by that number of kanban. In this machining line, parts *a* and *b* are both withdrawn, but these parts are produced according to the detached order of the production-ordering kanban.

Fine-Tuning Production. Let's consider fine-tuning production by using a kanban. Assume that an engine manufacturing process must produce 100 engines a day. The subsequent process requests 5 engines per one-time lot via a withdrawal kanban. These lots are then picked up 20 times a day, which amounts to a daily production of exactly 100 engines.

If we need to decrease all processes by 10 percent to fine-tune our production planning, this example's final process will have to withdraw engines 18 times a day. Then, since the engine process produces only 90 units a day, working hours will be reduced by the time needed to produce the 10 now-unneeded units. On the other hand, if we need to increase production quantities by 10 percent, the final process must withdraw engines 22 times a day with the kanban. The preceding process then has to produce 110 units, these additional 10 units being covered by overtime.

Although the Toyota production system is based on the assumption that units can be produced without any slack or unnecessary stock by regarding all human resources, machines, and materials as perfect, the risk of variations in production needs still exists. This risk is countered by paying overtime and encouraging improvement activities at each process.

Production Leveling. Production leveling is the most important condition of kanban-inspired production for minimizing slack time in terms of workforce, equipment, and work-in-process. It is the cornerstone of the Toyota production system.

As described previously, the subsequent process goes to the preceding processes to withdraw goods needed, when needed, and in the quantities needed. If the subsequent process fluctuates its withdrawal of parts in terms of time or quantity, then the preceding process should prepare the inventory, equipment, and workforce that will be necessary to adapt to the highest variance of quantities demanded. Where there are many sequential processes, the variance of quantities withdrawn by each subsequent process may increase as we move further back along the preceding processes. To prevent such large variances in all production lines, including those of a company's subcontractors, an effort must be made to minimize production fluctuation in the final assembly line. Therefore, as Toyota's final process, the finished car assembly line will convey each type of automobile in the smallest possible lot size to achieve the ideal of one-piece production and flow. The line, in turn, will receive needed parts in their small-lot sizes from the preceding processes.

In short, production leveling minimizes the variation in the withdrawal quantities of parts produced at each subassembly, thereby allowing the subassemblies to produce each part at a constant speed, or at a fixed quantity per hour. Such a production leveling is illustrated by the following example.

Suppose a production line is required to produce 10,000 Toyota Coronas in 20 eight-hour operating days. The 10,000 Coronas consist of 5,000 sedans, 2,500 hardtops, and 2,500 wagons. Dividing these numbers by 20 operating days results in 250 sedans, 125 hardtops, and 125 wagons per day; this levels the average daily production of each car type. During an eight-hour operating shift (480 minutes), all 500 units must be produced. Therefore, the "unit cycle time," or average time required to produce one vehicle of any type, is 0.96 minutes (480 ÷ 500), or approximately 57.5 seconds.

The proper mix, or production sequence, can be determined by comparing the cycle time needed to produce one vehicle of any type with the maximum time permitted to produce a specific Corona model. For example, the maximum time needed to produce one Corona sedan is determined by dividing the shift time (480 minutes) by the number of sedans to be produced in the shift (250); in this case, the maximum time is 1 minute, 55 seconds. This means a sedan must and will be generated every 1 minute, 55 seconds. Comparing this time interval with the cycle time of 57.5 seconds, it is obvious that another car type could be produced between the time one sedan is completed and another must be produced. So, the basic sequence is sedan, other, sedan, other, and so on.

The maximum time needed to produce a wagon or hardtop is 3 minutes, 50 seconds (480 ÷ 125). Comparing this figure with the cycle time of 57.5 seconds, it is obvious that three cars of any type can be produced between each wagon or hardtop. If a wagon follows the first sedan in production, then the production sequence would be sedan, wagon, sedan, hardtop, sedan, wagon, sedan, hardtop, and so on. This is an example of leveling the production of a variety of products.

When considering manufacturing equipment, a conflict arises between product variety and production leveling. When producing a smaller variety of products, specialized equipment for mass production can be a powerful weapon for reducing costs. Toyota, however, has numerous car types in various combinations of model, tires, options, color, and so forth. For example, 3,000 or 4,000 kinds of Coronas are being produced. To promote leveled production in such a variety of products, it is necessary to have general-purpose or flexible machines. By using a minimal number of instruments and tools on these machines, Toyota's specialized production processes accommodate the efficiency of these machines.

An advantage of leveled production's response to product variety is that the system can adapt smoothly to fluctuating customer demands by gradually changing the frequency of lots without altering the lot size in each process. This is fine-tuning production using kanban. To achieve leveled production, reducing production lead time will be necessary to produce various product types promptly. Minimizing lot sizes, in turn, will require reducing lead times for setup.

Setup Problems. The most difficult point in promoting smooth production is setup. In a pressing process, for example, common sense dictates that costs can be reduced by continuously using one type of die, thereby producing large lot sizes and reducing setup costs. However, when the final process has averaged its production and reduced the stocks between the punch press and its subsequent body line, the pressing department as a preceding process must make frequent and rapid setups. This means frequently altering the die types corresponding to the greater variety of products being withdrawn by the subsequent process.

At Toyota, from 1945 to 1954, the pressing department's setup time had been two or three hours. It was reduced to a quarter hour in the years 1955 to 1964, and to only three minutes after 1970.

To shorten setup times, it is important to prepare neatly in advance the necessary jigs, tools, the next die, and materials, and to remove the detached die and jigs after the new die is set and the machine begins to operate. This phase of setup actions is called the "external" setup. The worker should concentrate on actions needed while the machine is stopping. This phase of setup actions is called the "internal" setup. It is crucial to convert as much internal setup as possible to external setup.

Process Design. Consider the design or layout of processes in a plant. Each of five stands of lathes, milling machines, and drilling machines are laid out side by side, with one worker assigned to each machine so that a turner handles only a lathe. In the Toyota production system, the layout of machines is rearranged to smooth the production flow. One worker, therefore, might handle three types of machines (for example, a lathe, milling machine, and drilling machine) at the same time. This system is called *multiprocess handling*. In other words, the single-skilled worker, a concept which prevailed previously in Toyota plants, has become a *multiskilled worker*.

In a multiprocess-handling line, a worker handles several machines of various processes one by one. Work at each process will proceed only when the worker completes his or her given jobs within a cycle time. As a result, the introduction of each unit to the line is balanced by the completion of another unit of finished product, as ordered by the operations of a cycle time. This is called one-piece production and conveyance production. This rearrangement produces the following benefits:

- It eliminates unnecessary inventory between each process.
- It decreases the number of workers required and increases the line's productivity.
- As workers become multiskilled, they can participate in the total system of a plant and feel greater job satisfaction.
- By becoming multiskilled, workers can work in teams and help each other.

The concept of multiskilled workers is Japanese. In U.S. and European companies, many different labor unions co-exist in a single plant. A turner, for example, handles only a lathe and usually will not work on any other kind of machine. In Japan, on the other hand, only one union exists in each company, which facilitates worker mobility. Obviously, this difference may pose a major obstacle for U.S. and European companies wishing to adopt the Toyota production system.

Job Standardization. Toyota's standard operations differ from the usual operations in that they mainly show the sequential routine of various operations overseen by a multiskilled worker handling multiple kinds of machines. Two kinds of sheets show standard operations: (1) the standard operations routine sheet, which looks like the usual worker-machine chart, and (2) the standard operations sheet, which is displayed in the plant for all workers to see. The latter sheet specifies the cycle time, standard operations routine, and standard quantity of the work in process.

Cycle time or *takt* time is the standard specified number of minutes and seconds in which each line must produce one product or part. Cycle time refers to the production capability based on current manpower, while takt time refers to what the market demands. This is computed using the following formulas (the necessary output per month is predetermined from the demand side):

$$\text{Required daily output} = \frac{\text{required monthly output}}{\text{operating days per month}}$$

$$\text{Cycle time} = \frac{\text{daily operating hours}}{\text{required daily output}}$$

Once a month, the central planning office will inform each production department of this required daily quantity and the cycle time. In turn, each process manager will determine the number of workers required to produce one unit of output in a cycle time for this process. The plant's entire workforce must then be repositioned to reduce the operation rate of each process to a minimum number of workers.

Kanban are not the only sources of information given to each process. A kanban is a type of production-dispatching information during the month in question, whereas the daily quantity and cycle time information are given in advance to prepare the plantwide master production schedule.

The standard operations routine indicates the operations sequence that should be followed by a worker handling multiple processes. This is the work order to pick up the material, put it on the machine, and remove it after processing. This operations order continues for the various machines handled. Line balancing can be achieved among workers in this department because they will finish all their operations within the cycle time.

The standard quantity of work-in-process (WIP) is the minimum quantity of work being processed within a production line. This includes the work attached to machines. Without this quantity of work, the predetermined sequence of various kinds of machines in the whole line cannot operate simultaneously. Theoretically, however, if the invisible conveyor belt is achieved in this line, there is no need for WIP inventory.

Autonomation. As noted previously, the two pillars that support the Toyota production system are just-in-time and autonomation. To achieve perfect JIT, all the units flowing to the subsequent process must be defect-free, and this flow must be rhythmic and without interruption. Therefore, quality control must co-exist with the JIT operation throughout the kanban system. Autonomation means building into a mechanism the means to prevent mass-producing defects in machines or production lines. The word "autonomation" is not automation, but the ability to respond to any abnormalities that occur in a process.

The autonomous machine is a machine to which an automatic stopping device is attached. Almost all Toyota machines are autonomous, preventing the mass-production of defects and automatically checking machine breakdowns. This so-called mistake-proofing *(poka-yoke)* system is one mechanism that prevents defects by putting checking devices on the tools and machines.

Autonomation also extends to manual production lines. If something abnormal occurs in a production line, the worker pushes a stop button, thereby stopping the entire line. At Toyota, the *andon* system is important in performing this autonomous check, and it is an example of Toyota's visual control system (VCS). For the purpose of troubleshooting in each process, an electric light board, or *andon*, indicating a line stop is hung high enough in a plant to be seen easily by everyone. When a worker needs help adjusting to a job delay, he or she turns on the yellow light. If the worker needs the line stopped to make a machine adjustment, the red light is turned on. In summary, autonomation is a mechanism that autonomously checks anything unusual in a process.

Improvement Activities. The Toyota production system integrates and attains different goals such as quantity control, quality assurance, and respect for the worker while pursuing its ultimate goal of reducing costs. The process by which all these goals are realized is improvement activities, a fundamental element of the Toyota system. Each worker has the opportunity to make suggestions and propose improvements via small groups called QC circles. This suggestion-making process encourages improvements in quantity control by adapting standard operations routines to changes in cycle time; in quality assurance by preventing recurrence of defective works and machines; and, lastly, in respect for the worker by allowing each worker to participate in the production process.

Conclusion. The basic purpose of the Toyota production system is to increase profits by reducing costs — that is, by completely eliminating waste such as excessive inventory or workforce. The concept of costs in this context is broad. It is essentially the past, present, or future cash outlay deducted from sales revenue to attain a profit. Therefore, costs include not only manufacturing costs (reduced by cutting the workforce), but also administrative, capital (reduced by inventory cuts), and sales costs. To achieve cost reduction, production must promptly and flexibly adapt to changes in market demand without having wasteful slacks. This ideal is accomplished through just-in-time, producing the necessary items in the necessary quantities at the necessary time. At Toyota, the kanban system has been developed to facilitate production during a month and manage JIT. To implement the kanban system, production must be smoothed to level both quantities and variety in the withdrawal of parts by the final assembly line. Such leveling will require reducing the production lead time because various parts must be produced promptly each day. This can be attained by small-lot or one-piece production and conveyance. Small-lot production can be achieved through shortened setup times, and one-piece production achieved by the multiskilled workers of the multiprocess holding line. Standard operations routines will ensure the completion of all jobs necessary to process one unit of a product in a cycle time. The JIT production of 100 percent defect-free products will be ensured by autonomation (autonomous defect control systems). Finally, improvement activities will contribute to the overall process by modifying standard operations, eliminating defects, and, finally, by raising worker morale.

Where have these basic ideas come from? What need evoked them? They are believed to have come from the market constraints that characterized the Japanese automobile industry in postwar days: great variety within small production quantities. After 1950, Toyota thought it would be dangerous to blindly imitate the Ford system, which minimized the average unit cost by producing large quantities. American mass production techniques were effective in the high-growth period, which lasted until 1973. In the low-growth period that followed the oil crisis, however, the Toyota production system attracted more attention and was adopted by many industries in Japan to increase profit by decreasing costs and waste.

The Toyota production system is a unique, revolutionary system. The only problems Western companies may have in adopting it are labor unions and unfamiliarity with the multiskilled worker concept. They might encounter difficulties if the system is applied only partially. Many Japanese companies are already using it in its imperfect and its perfect form. The kanban system and production leveling could be particularly important to the West. To implement fully the Toyota system, upper management must proceed through the bargaining process with unions, a process often experienced by many Japanese companies as well.

5

Cost Accounting and Cost Control in the Just-In-Time Production System: The Daihatsu Experience*

The topic of this chapter is the relationship between the just-in-time (JIT) system and cost accounting and cost control, a relationship that has been the topic of a number of case studies published in the United States. Despite interest in Japan, however, there has been almost no empirical research done there on the topic. Given the fact that Japan gave birth to the JIT production system, it would appear that case studies, questionnaires, and the like, directed at Japanese firms would serve a useful purpose. Thus, while it may only scratch the surface, this chapter will present a case study of Daihatsu Motor Company and some observations on its cost accounting and cost control systems as they have developed under the JIT production system. The information presented has been gathered with the company's cooperation.

In an effort to become acquainted with the main problems in this field, we will consider first the evidence available from the

---

* Translated with permission from *Kogyō kaikei* (Business Accounting Journal), 40, No. 5 (1988).

United States concerning cost accounting and cost control under the
JIT production system. We will then look at the Japanese situation
as revealed in a question-and-answer format with Daihatsu personnel. Finally, we will present a short summary of the information collected.

The U.S. Situation. In a study of Hewlett-Packard, Hunt and
Merz[1] list three ways in which the company's JIT system has affected its cost accounting system:

1. JIT has eliminated the direct labor cost category and
   incorporated it as indirect production costs.
2. The treatment of indirect production costs. It treats
   direct labor costs (processing costs) as a period
   expense and directly figures them as a part of sales
   costs.
3. JIT has reduced the role of cost accounting in failed
   and rework jobs.

These three points are summarized in Figure 5-1. As is evident,
their new simplified system is none other than a system, commonly
used in Japan, of integrated cost accounting by machine cost and
process.

Further, Boer describes a joint conference held with the National
Association of Accountants (NAA) on "Cost Accounting Robotics
and the New Manufacturing Environment."[2] The conference's 170
participants had just visited a Nissan plant. Boer summarized the
papers presented at this conference, particularly those dealing with
the JIT production system's influence on cost accounting and cost
control:

1. Labor costs have become an increasingly minor portion of overall manufacturing costs, and there is no
   particular need to apportion time directly for specific
   orders, products, or the like. (This suggests that there
   is no need to independently figure direct labor costs
   and directly calculate them as part of product costs.)
2. The traditional distinctions between manufacturing
   and support sections are becoming increasingly

Hewlett-Packard's Simplified System

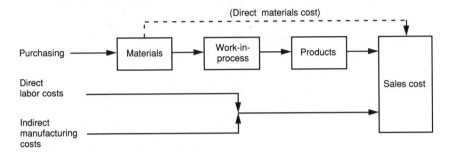

Traditional Product Cost Accounting System

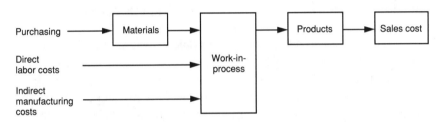

Figure 5-1. Cost Control Comparisons: Hewlett-Packard's Simplified System and the Traditional System

blurred because there is an increased tendency to consider service functions as part of the manufacturing process. For example, direct labor by itself is a part of machine maintenance.

3. A simplified accounting system is a prerequisite for a simplified plant.

4. When workers are considered part of the management team, reform activities tend to be conducted autonomously. Detailed accounting control procedures are therefore not only impractical, but a waste of time as well.

5. Inventories perform the undesirable role of hiding a variety of management control problems.

6. It is necessary to recognize the numerous factors that can influence cost standards and to control them. (It is important to note that we are not speaking here of monetary, dollar-figure costs, but rather of target management control of the various factors influencing costs after they have been broken down.)

Points 4 and 6 of Boer's summary deserve special attention. The reasoning here is that there is a growing tendency to believe that applying accounting controls is impractical or even redundant. What is important, however, is to control the physical elements of production that can influence cost standards. Cost control in this sense implies workplace reforms. It is now believed that the JIT production system is crucial to this type of workplace reform.

Daihatsu's Cost Accounting and Cost Reform System. The information in this section was provided during the course of an interview conducted July 13, 1987, at Daihatsu corporate headquarters with Shigeaki Fukamori, head of the cost accounting department, and Kagahiko Yoshioka, head of the cost planning section. The results are reported in a question-and-answer format. Additional information is drawn from an earlier article written by the author in conjunction with a member of Daihatsu's board of directors and head of the purchasing department.[3]

Question 1: According to a recent issue of the U.S. journal *Management Accounting*, Hewlett-Packard's use of the just-in-time kanban system has resulted in changes in its cost accounting practices. Using the JIT system has shrunk the company's inventory levels considerably, reducing the time required from the start of production to shipment of the finished product. This means that indirect manufacturing costs — including direct labor costs, or what we might call processing costs — can now be included in the monthly sales costs. In other words, processing costs are now treated as quarterly expenses charged directly to sales costs. Processing costs, including those for finished goods or work-in-process inventoried at the end of the quarter, are then adjusted at the end of the quarter. Since Daihatsu has adopted the Toyota production system in all facets of its organization, I want to know if you have seen changes like this in your cost accounting practices.

Answer: Even before we adopted the Toyota system, we were using a system similar to the just-in-time format. It's true, however, that our inventory levels went down when we introduced the kanban system. Our year's inventory levels do not fluctuate much, but even so, this has not caused any basic changes in our cost accounting system.

Like Hewlett-Packard, Daihatsu uses direct costing as part of its management accounting. This allows us to carry fixed costs as direct quarterly expenses although we don't calculate direct labor costs as quarterly expenses. Direct labor costs are variable expenses when factors such as overtime and part-time labor are calculated.

Question 2: The trend toward automated factories has grown lately. At companies such as Hewlett-Packard, it has become the practice to eliminate direct labor costs as an expense item, calculating them as part of the indirect manufacturing costs. This allows them to reduce direct labor costs to between 3 and 5 percent of manufacturing costs. Do you follow this practice at Daihatsu?

Answer: We combine direct labor costs with indirect manufacturing costs and treat them as processing costs.

Question 3: If you eliminate the direct labor costs by combining them with indirect costs to be treated as processing costs, then it seems only natural to assume that direct labor costs themselves would not be calculated on individual products. They would be treated differently than direct materials costs. Is that the case? How do you calculate the processing costs of individual products?

Answer: Direct labor costs are calculated with indirect costs and are shifted to individual product cost accounts through departmental cost accounts. In other words, we establish a rate for distributing processing costs among the individual departments. At the same time, each department establishes standard times for the manufacture of each of its products and for each model vehicle. We use these to figure standard processing costs for individual products or vehicle models, costs that are calculated as a part of each individual product's cost accounting. We do not calculate direct labor costs independently and treat them the way we treat direct material costs — we do not factor direct labor costs immediately into individual product costs the same way we factor in direct material costs. Instead, we combine them with indirect costs and first calculate them as part of the costs for the individual departments. We have used this system for some time at Daihatsu. Direct labor costs, as always, carry considerable weight within processing costs.

Question 4: Another trend in this period of increased automation is that the amount of direct machining or processing is dropping, while the time spent on indirect machining is rising. I suppose this is true in Japan as well. One influence of this on cost accounting systems is that emphasis is shifted from worker rates to machine rates. This gives us a more accurate picture of costs. What can you tell us about this trend at Daihatsu?

Answer: We have seen the same trends here. Automation has proceeded apace at the engine unit plant at our Takio manufacturing facility, for example, and parts are made in one-minute cycles. Nearly all machining there is automated now, so we have started using a machine rate. Also, because a considerable amount of press work is automated, we have established a machine rate for each punch. Automation is now progressing in the machining divisions, shifting us to machine rates there.

But in other areas, such as automotive assembly, painting, and mounting engines and other parts, we still determine standard times for each model vehicle or each part based on our old formula of cycle time multiplied by number of workers. The cycle time for these divisions is the same as the cycle time for the conveyor. And even in our machining divisions, we have established standard times for individual automobiles based on the formula of machining cycle time multiplied by number of workers. So you can see that, in the automotive industry, the worker rate still carries considerable weight. Cycle time is calculated from demand during the month in question and is the amount of time needed to manufacture one model vehicle or one part. It is calculated for each individual process. At automotive plants, we are normally dealing with short time spans of one or two minutes.

Question 5: A legacy of the just-in-time system at companies such as Hewlett-Packard is that many cost reforms are now being implemented. This means that accounting control measures, such as variance analysis based on standard cost accounting procedures, are not only no longer practical, they are even a waste of time. Workers are now organized into small groups, such as quality control circles, and autonomously carry out continuous incremental improvements, which then become the cost controls for the workplace. Have you seen this at Daihatsu?

Answer: An accountant hearing the words "continuous incremental cost improvements" tends to think of cost control systems based on standard cost accounting. Cost control activities undertaken at Daihatsu, however, have not been based on standard cost accounting systems. Working outside these systems, as part of our overall budget control system, we have seen (1) reforms based on material resource levels (labor hour controls and controls affected by kanban) and (2) reforms at the departmental and expense item level.

We started using the standard cost accounting system at Daihatsu in 1957. At the end of each month, we would calculate items, such as variations between budgeted funds and funds actually spent in each division, variations between ideal and actual productivity rates, operational variations, and so on. But now we have given up balancing these accounts and are using the standard cost accounting system primarily for financial accounting. The reason we conduct cost reforms outside the standard cost accounting system is not because we take these reforms less seriously — rather, it is because they are very important to us. The standard cost is limited by financial accounting restrictions, which means it is sometimes inappropriate for us to explain physical differences as part of the management system. This is reflected by the fact that material level standards, such as processing time for each product, and materials costs tend to balance out over the course of a year.

So at Daihatsu, we distinguish between standard cost and target cost. In fact, we control our manufacturing activities on the basis of target cost. For example, even with the standard cost accounting system currently used at Daihatsu, we determine the standard time for parts or individual vehicle models in terms of each department's costs. We then multiply this by the processing cost distribution rate assumed by the department in question to determine standard processing costs for each part and model vehicle. These standard times are done annually for each department. In the assembly department, we average out the number of workers and the conveyor time over a year and use this figure in our calculations, the same figure over the entire year.

We have a similar practice for purchased parts. We use the actual price for the parts paid at the end of the previous quarter to determine standard costs. For parts we make in-house, we calculate a standard cost based on the plant's average capacity, taking into consideration factors such as the degree of skilled labor or level of automation. These standard cost figures are maintained over the course of an entire year, which enables us to estimate yearly averages. We also have a rule of rounding off the basic unit.

Concerning the standard times for each department, it should be noted that the target value for the month to come is derived by multiplying the cycle time by the number of workers for the current month, which means the target figures will differ monthly. Because of what the Toyota production system calls process job reforms, the number generally decreases slightly each month. The basic unit for labor hours is derived by multiplying the cycle time by the number of workers working directly on the job in question. The targeted number of labor hours is calculated by applying a valuative measure to the number of labor hours determined as already explained, then figuring in the targeted reduction rate from the profitability plan. A reduction target line is then plotted for each month from the first to last quarter.

In months when the predicted production level is high, either overtime is increased or the cycle time is shortened and direct labor is increased as necessary to cover the work to be done. These are the only ways we have of dealing with busy months. We do attempt, however, to pool all the knowledge and experience present in the plant to institute job reforms to keep increases in direct labor to a minimum. Conversely, we can allocate people within the range established by the formula of multiplying targeted worker hours by the estimated production quantity, then perform as many job reforms as necessary to reach the targeted production level for the month. At Toyota, this is called worker savings.

Question 6: Are you saying that the use of accounting controls is decreasing at Daihatsu?

Answer: We unquestionably use quantity-based controls in our plants, but fundamentally we use financial-type monetary controls. To begin with, we formulate quarterly profitability plans, expressed in cash terms. These are used to determine the target costs for the coming year. (Cost equals the target cost for the quarter divided by the anticipated production quantity.) The target for the direct cost of products is broken down for each shop in the plant as a cost target figure.

Our budget period is for one year, but only the first six months are really set up with precision. The second half of the year is comparatively loose. We use the rolling method to correct the six-month periods. In fact, you can think of our targeted reduction rates as applied in six-month cycles.

The base figures multiplied by the targeted reduction rate are the targeted costs from the cost plan as applied to new products. These levels are expected to be attained within three months from the time production begins on new products. After that, these figures are also subject to reductions and are multiplied by the targeted reduction rate from the profitability plan to determine the new target costs for the coming year. From the second year on, the figures from the end of the previous year are used as the base that is multiplied by the targeted reduction rate.

Materials, paint, indirect materials, energy, direct labor, and other fluctuating costs at the factory are controlled by setting reduction target figures for each vehicle model. The purchasing department supervises pricing controls for materials, paints, and other items purchased from outside. The primary activities conducted at the plant include adding value to purchased items and using conservation measures to reduce consumption. Control measures taken for direct labor costs include quantitative controls and control of labor hours.

The target values for each month are called rationalization targets (or reduction targets). The target values for in-house items such as labor hours and the like are set each month. Our general rule, however, is to attain departmental expenses, such as expenditure budgets, over a three-month period or to evaluate them in terms of average figures taken over a six-month period. Items from the fixed costs line are subjected to target controls based on overall cash reduction targets and not to these per-vehicle reduction target controls. This, in itself, is a budgetary restriction.

Monthly targets for direct labor costs in the profitability plan are converted at the plant level to labor hour controls; the act of reaching these goals is known as target control. Certain aspects of the concept of efficiency variance set out in standard cost accounting are difficult for workers in the plant to understand. Even in a classification such as labor hours control, if you simply take the difference between targeted labor hours and actual labor hours and multiply this by the labor hour rate, you can immediately see what is meant by efficiency variance. In any event, you can say that variance analysis as found in standard cost accounting has been pushed to the background in this process. The target control system now predominates because it comes in the form of labor hour controls, which are easy for the supervisors and plant workers to understand. This increases efficiency in our attempts to lower costs.

Question 7: Hewlett-Packard and other U.S. firms have found that measures such as the JIT system or total quality control have cut their defectives rate, which in turn has reduced the amount of rework required. This results in less need for cost accounting regarding losses or rework. Is this true at Daihatsu?

Answer: The thoroughness of our quality control program has led to considerably fewer job-related defects than before. When we do have failed job problems, they are more likely caused by defective materials. The role that failed jobs play in costs has also been reduced. Even so, however, it would not be true to say that this has brought about changes in our cost accounting system.

Question 8: The competition in product development among home appliance manufacturers — particularly makers of electronics products — is quite fierce and, consequently, product life cycles are now extremely short. Companies are forced to come out yearly with

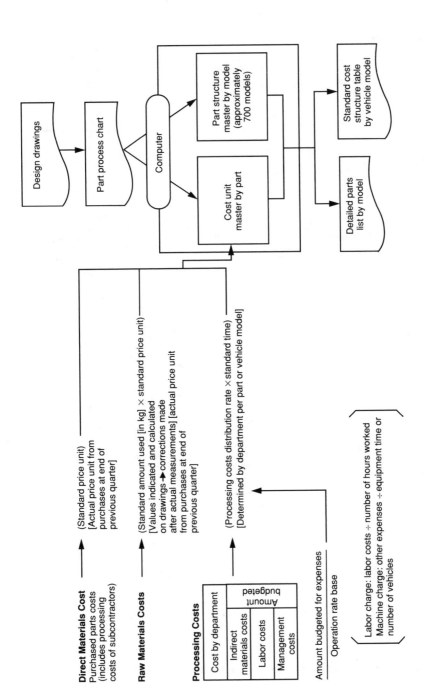

Figure 5-2. Standard Procedures for Setting Cost (Automotive)

Direct Materials Costs

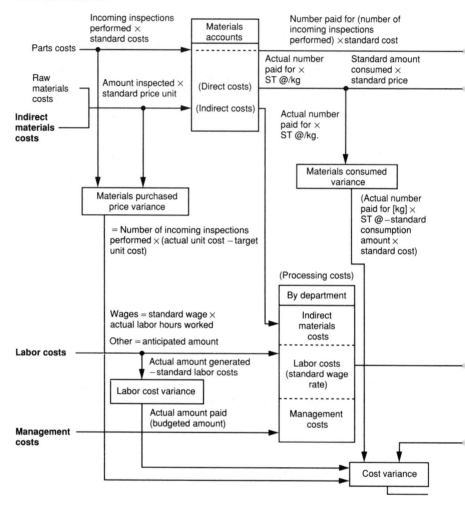

Figure 5-3. Administration of Standard Cost Accounting System (Automotive)

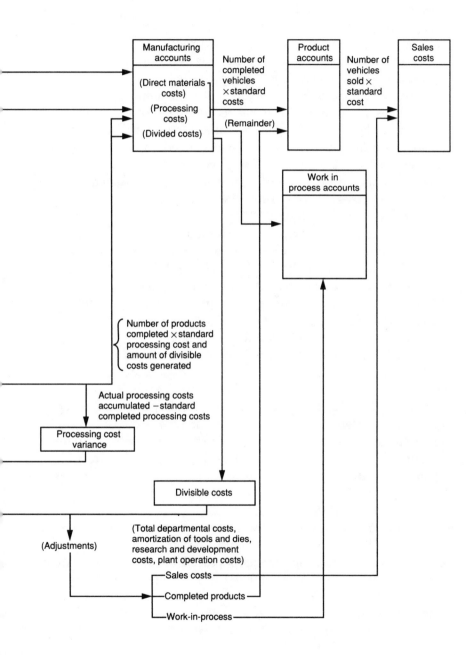

new models for each of their products. Of course, companies want to recover their development costs as early as possible. To do this, they calculate development costs as part of product costs when pricing the product. In financial accounting, this is dropped into quarterly expenses. Does Daihatsu follow this practice?

Answer: Research and development costs are inevitably treated as fixed costs in terms of financial accounting, but when we set our target costs, however, they are treated as plan-related costs and calculated into the product cost. By plan-related costs, we mean that they will be objects of control during cost planning. Common fixed costs, such as amortization of general-purpose equipment, are not plan-related costs. The costs for developing prototypes used to be treated as common fixed costs. They are now calculated into the target costs as special fixed costs for each model.

The significance of considering design and development costs as plan-related costs, and hence a part of the target costs, is that we can calculate the total design and development labor hours (estimated labor hours times rate) to make them part of the target costs. This allows us to treat design and development costs in a way that can be controlled by the product manager.

The Daihatsu cost accounting system is outlined in Figures 5-2 and 5-3.

Conclusion. Based on this study, it can safely be said that the JIT production system has had little impact on standard cost accounting procedures as it pertains to financial accounting, or on actual cost accounting systems, at least insofar as this system is practiced at Daihatsu. As one of the most powerful members of the Toyota group of companies, Daihatsu is one of the primary practitioners of the Toyota production system.

Even so, the standard cost control system no longer has the importance it once had in cost control because, under the JIT production system, more emphasis is placed on physically oriented target control systems implemented in the workplace. Although it does not represent a retreat of financially oriented or management accounting types of management control systems, it must be perceived as part of the proliferation of financial control directives and the target control system.

6

An Integrated System of MRP, Kanban, and Cost Accounting

Computer-assisted decision-making support systems are producing major changes in the fields of production control and cost accounting. Standard cost accounting systems based on computer techniques for production control include materials requirement planning (MRP) developed in the United States and the Toyota production system and the kanban (or sign) method developed in Japan. Although the use of computers is indispensable for the use of kanban, this method is not in opposition to MRP, and many Japanese companies use both methods.

MRP and kanban methods can be used together to ensure product control. In addition to planning functions, they also provide complementary functions. Furthermore, since an MRP database incorporates a database for cost accounting, it is also possible to integrate a production control system with cost control and profit control systems in the form of a database.

While this chapter concentrates on MRP, it also examines systems that represent an integration of MRP, kanban, and cost accounting.[1]

Three Methods of Production Control. There are three production control methods used by Japanese companies: the *seiban* or product number method, MRP, and the kanban method.

The Seiban Method. The seiban method uses a parts composition list to calculate both the quantity of parts and material needed and the product cost. However, this is not the multistage parts list used with MRP. It is a list of basic unit prices (quick deck) that disregards the stratification of parts composition.

Parts are prepared using this list of basic unit prices, the needed quantities based on the number of customer orders received. With the seiban method, the written order sheet covers parts and materials that are calculated only in needed quantities together with the assigned product numbers of the parts. A number indicates the production book number of the part. For example, if the product number of an ordered product X is 110, then parts A, B, and C that are required for this product will be assigned the number 110 on the order sheet.

One disadvantage of the seiban method becomes obvious when the production plan changes; for instance, when it becomes necessary to change the assigned number of 50 units of purchased part A from 110 to 111. In this case, because a different product number is assigned to the same type of part, delivery control of part A becomes impossible.

Materials Requirement Planning. In MRP, production book numbers (for instance, 110) are assigned to an order for final product X. In this respect, the method is similar to the seiban method. Rather than using a parts composition list, however, MRP calculates the quantity of parts needed at each production stage on a multistage parts list.

Product numbers for the final product are assigned to each level of parts according to the production book numbers (for instance, 1,000). This method is less labor-intensive when it becomes necessary to modify numbers assigned to the same type of part. Controlling the delivery of parts at each production stage also becomes more flexible when coping with fluctuations in basic production planning. Instead, the remaining inventory and equipment are subtracted according to calculations of the net quantity required for each part, which is handy for accurate inventory updates.[2] The problem with cost accounting is that when the product number of a final product is calculated using the seiban method, the same number is assigned to all of its related parts. Thus, a separate cost accounting system is employed. In the case of MRP, parts are treated independently from the final product so that calculating the product cost includes production costs of the product at each stage. This is interpreted according to the standard parts list (or bill of materials) as the standard or estimated price.

The Kanban Method. The kanban method can be explained simply. Following final assembly, product B is placed in empty carrying containers. These containers are then transported to the subsequent downstream process, their contents marked with a sign or card *(kanban)* attached to each container. As containers of product B are emptied, they are collected at regular intervals along with their kanban cards and returned to the preceding process's storage area to await more finished product B. The cycle begins again with kanban-labeled containers of product B being transported from the storage area to the next downstream process.

Kanban cards placed in empty containers serve as productivity indicators in the preceding upstream cycle. With this method, needed parts are provided only when the downstream processes require them, or *just-in-time*. In JIT production, the amount of parts inventory that must be prepared in upstream cycles poses a problem. These quantities (plus the amount of inventory kept just to be safe) must equal the average demand amount and be restocked regularly.

This way of planning reduces the amount of inventory (that is, the output of the preceding upstream process plus the parts inventory needed for the subsequent downstream process). The time between restocking cycles can be shortened by one or two hours and allow for the delivery of goods several times daily. This makes smaller lot sizes possible, standardizes the daily number of small lot deliveries, and eliminates large amounts of inventory piling up at the final process.

For example, we see in Figure 6-1[3] that products A, B, C, and D used to be produced in large lots of 2,000 units: product A on day 1, product B on day 2, product C on day 3, and so on. With standardized (or leveled) production, 800 units of product A are produced daily — along with 600 units of product B, 400 units of product C, and 200 units of product D. In other words, they have standardized production of each product on a daily basis, making it possible to maintain a constant flow.

The Relationship between Production Systems and Production Control Methods. Can we use the three production control methods we've discussed irrespective of the production system to which these methods are applied? Is it possible to use multiple production methods within the same production system — or should we use only one? For instance, does the kanban method leave room for improvement and further innovation in a particular plant? To find the answers, we will examine five production systems and their relationships.

Production System #1: Large Lots and Anticipated Wide Variety. In an industry such as home electronics manufacturing with a broad customer base, the production system is market-oriented to sell large volumes. Because the demand is for large quantities of a wide variety of products, it is possible to determine daily standardized production levels if the monthly product volume is divided by the number of work days (for example, 25 days). Here, we can apply the kanban method and simultaneously use MRP.

A prerequisite for the kanban method, however, is to shorten the production lead time when the production plan changes. Consequently, single changeover (changeover in less than ten minutes) would be difficult to implement, for instance, in the iron and steel industries, the oil industry, fertilizer manufacturers, and glass, chemical, and pharmaceutical plants. For this particular production system, the kanban method is less meaningful and MRP is probably more effective.

Production System #2: Small Lots and Anticipated Wide Variety. With this system of production there is less demand for ensuring daily production levels for each product based on a monthly standard production plan. When the kanban method is

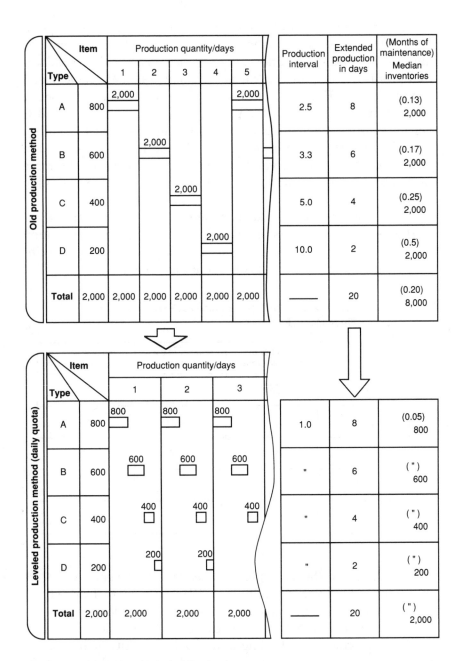

Figure 6-1. Examples of Leveled Production

applied, repeated multiple delivery of kanban and related operations will be necessary. This will require personnel for an increased
number of working operations. For instance, imagine that standardized production requires products A, B, and C hourly on October 1
and products D, E, and F on October 2. This means that on October 1
the kanban cards used for the production of products A, B, and C
will be returned to the place of manufacturing; on October 2, kanban
cards for the production of products D, E, and F will be returned to
the plant. Thus, when a variety of products is being made, more
cards and delivery operations are required at the plant, complicating
the work flow.

The critical point in the kanban method is its cost per number of
work operations. This cost is possible to verify using a simulation
based on a numerical formula. Let us consider the number of specifications and manufactured cars at Toyota (see Table 6-1).[4]

Table 6-1. Specifications and Cars Produced at Toyota during a
Three-Month Period

	Number of specifications	Number of cars produced	Number of cars per specification
Car A	3,700	63,000	17
Car B	16,400	204,000	12
Car C	4,500	53,000	12
Car D	7,500	44,000	6
Total	32,100	364,000	11

According to this example, between six and seventeen cars are
manufactured from each specification. We also know that some types
of cars are produced in small quantities and utilize a large number of
parts. Given the fact that automobiles are usually considered a mass-
produced product, it is startling how small a quantity is involved in
this instance. This is why, according to the group technology (GT)

method, a variety of standardized parts can be assembled in different ways to manufacture different types of final products.

Consequently, even when discussing standardized production, we do not mean that an average monthly production figure is required for this standardization. In many automobile manufacturers, short time spans of one or two hours are often required for multiple cycles during the production of parts, and standardizing the production of products X, Y, Z, or W is often common hourly in the course of a single day.

Thus, even when the production of products P, Q, R, and S is standardized hourly during the course of a different period on the same day, only rarely must different kanban cards be resupplied to the plant depending on the time of day. This is because it is possible to simultaneously use a variety of parts of products X, Y, Z, and W and of products P, Q, R, and S because they have been standardized. Specifications for a group of parts used at the same time will only differ for different types of products. However, it would probably be imprudent to say that the kanban method is efficient in automobile manufacturing.

Innovative activity in manufacturing plants has led to the development of kanban arrangement boards for subsequent processes. All cards that refer to various types of parts are posted. Because the number of work operations is not that high, with this arrangement it is possible to take down cards that are being used for manufactured products if the types of manufactured products are changed in subsequent cycles during the course of a month. On the other hand, if it were not for the increased standardization and joint use of parts, the number of work operations accompanying the use of cards would grow so much that the MRP method would be indispensable.

One way to apply the kanban method is to use it with MRP. A specific feature is that the kanban method is based on small-lot and single-line production, making the lot composition almost useless. Since it is also based on standardized production, the lead time shifts to accommodate the start day of production. (This point will be illustrated later.)

Production System #3: Large Lots that Vary in Size. For our purposes we will exclude those subcontractors that are affiliated with specific companies and concentrate on those independent manufacturers that rely on orders from numerous businesses.

Since lot sizes vary on individual large orders, standardizing basic production is often possible. For instance, automotive parts manufacturers who order from external subcontractors find it possible to use the kanban method. In cases where standardized production poses problems, only MRP can be used. When standardization is possible, however, it is possible to use both MRP and the kanban method.

Production System #4: Lot Sizes that Vary from Small to Large. Here we discuss independent manufacturers again, this time, however, with a look at those companies that receive orders in both large and small quantities.

This manufacturing environment makes it impossible to ensure a standard daily volume even for one-month periods. In such cases

Table 6-2. Relationship between the Production System and the Production Control Method

---

(1) Large-lot wide-variety production

  a) Assembly and machinery industry .... joint use of kanban and MRP

  b) Equipment industry (chemical industry) .... MRP only

(2) Small-lot wide-variety production

  a) With a high degree of standardization and joint use of parts and in cases where standardized production of parts is possible .... joint use of kanban and MRP

  b) With a low degree of standardization and joint use of parts, and in cases when modification of the kanban method would lead to a great number of job operations .... MRP only

(3) Production for large lots that vary in size

  a) In cases when production standardization is possible ....joint use of kanban and MRP

  b) In cases when production standardization would be difficult...MRP only

(4) Small-lot production

  Same as (3), except that many cases will correspond to (3b)

(5) Production for individual orders

  Same as (3), except that even more cases will correspond to (3b)...joint use of MRP and seiban the kanban method is not applicable. On the other hand, if the manufacturer's parts are standardized and common to all orders, it becomes possible to ensure a certain volume of parts production. Thus, it is necessary to promote the standardized production of finished products according to principles for large-lot production. When the kanban method is not applicable, only MRP should be used.

Production System #5: When Orders Are for Individual Lots. Here, specification will vary depending on the machine tools, shipping industry requirements, and the like. There are also differences in the quantity of each order, making standardized production extremely difficult. Consequently, it is difficult to apply the kanban method. On the other hand, in the construction industry, when parts are standardized (as in the panel construction method's use of prefabricated parts), it is possible to standardize on-site construction parts obtained from previous processes. Nevertheless, with these production demands, MRP and the seiban method can be used jointly.

Table 6-2 summarizes this discussion.

An Outline of MRP's Required Quantity Planning. Although it has many subsystems, MRP's primary focus is on the required quantity cost accounting of materials and parts. Figures 6-2 and 6-3 use simple numerical examples to illustrate the basic data necessary for required quantity accounting. We will also explain this basic data and the sequential calculation steps involved, beginning with product X.

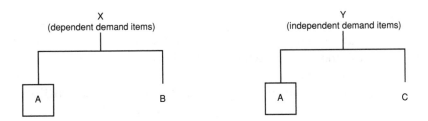

(Note) Both products X and Y use one part A.

Figure 6-2. Two Parts Lists

Master production schedule

Period	1	2	3	4	5	6	7	8	9	10
X			100	100	100	100	100	100	100	100
Y			150		150		150		150	

Part master data →	Policy for placing orders	Lead time
	X ... fixed quantity lot multiplication method (300 units) Y ... basic production plan items (independent demand) A ... fixed amount lot multiplication method (200 units)	2 periods 1 period 1 period

	Remaining inventory on hand (OH)	Remaining orders placed (remaining work-in-process, on order) (OO)		Already assigned	Spoilage ratio	Safe number
		Quantity	Lead time			
X	100	200	3	0	0	100
Y	200	200	2	0	0	0
A	150	100	1	80	6%	250

Figure 6-3. Master Production Schedule and Part Master Data

Using Data from the Master Production Schedule. The upper table of Figure 6-3 shows the master production schedule of product X. While the master production schedule can be a comprehensive daily plan of operations, often in Japan the comprehensive daily plan is determined in monthly units. In contrast, with MRP this determination is based on weekly or daily unit periods.

The master production schedule starts with the expected sales for the volume of production anticipated by the sales department. Then, the anticipated remaining inventory at the end of the month and at the beginning of the month is either added or subtracted to arrive at the production quantities. Corrections are made that take into account the number of workers and the capacity of equipment and material. In the final stage, once an agreement is reached with the sales department, a weekly or daily unit of product-specific demand quantities is determined.

This master production schedule does not represent a daily production schedule. The master production schedule is the result of production planning and is determined for respective lots. Its start date also takes the lead time into account.

Calculating the Overall Required Quantity. For now, the master production schedule for product X, shown in Figure 6-3, will input the overall required quantity in the first line of the daily production schedule table of product X (see the upper left section of Figure 6-4).

In addition, 100 units of product X are required as a safe inventory quantity according to the master plan (see "safe numbers" in Figure 6-3). The addition of safe numbers to the overall required quantity is done for advanced shipping with a lead time starting from period 1. Since the lead time for product X is 2, the quantity is added to period 3. The reason for adding advanced shipping is that only the lead time portion of the planned start day of production is restored. Once the safe numbers have been incorporated, the required quantity after incorporation is calculated.

Calculating the Net Required Quantity. Calculating the net required quantity is done by subtracting the amount of remaining inventory and the amount of work-in-process (WIP), or remaining orders, from the required quantity after incorporation. We see from the parts master data in Figure 6-3 that the current status of remaining inventory of product X (OH = on hand) is 100, the status of WIP/remaining products on order (OO = on order) is 200, and the delivery status period is 3. When this is entered into the table of the daily production plan, the inventory of 100 and 200 remaining products on order totals 300. For this total, the overall required quantity of 200 for period 3 and the overall required quantity of 100 for period 4 is sufficient. Consequently, each overall required quantity after period 5 will be the net required quantity.

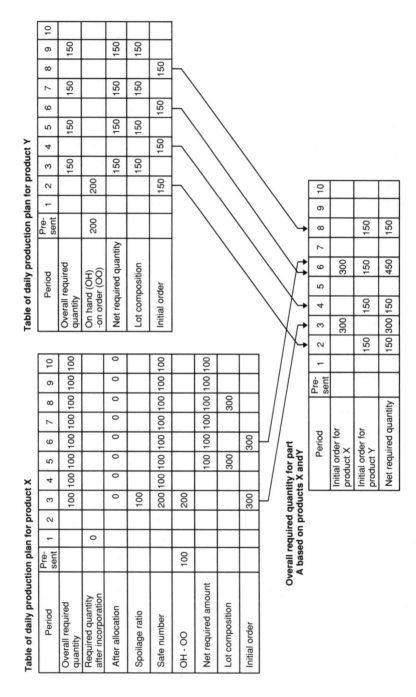

Table of daily production plan for product X

Period	Pre-sent	1	2	3	4	5	6	7	8	9	10
Overall required quantity				100	100	100	100	100	100	100	100
Required quantity after incorporation	0										
After allocation				0	0	0	0	0	0	0	0
Spoilage ratio				100							
Safe number				200	100	100	100	100	100	100	100
OH - OO	100		200								
Net required amount						100	100	100	100	100	100
Lot composition						300			300		
Initial order				300			300				

Table of daily production plan for product Y

Period	Pre-sent	1	2	3	4	5	6	7	8	9	10
Overall required quantity				150	150	150	150	150	150	150	
On hand (OH) -on order (OO)	200	200									
Net required quantity				150	150	150	150	150	150	150	
Lot composition				150	150	150	150	150	150		
Initial order			150	150							

Overall required quantity for part A based on products X and Y

Period	Pre-sent	1	2	3	4	5	6	7	8	9	10
Initial order for product X				300			300				
Initial order for product Y			150	150	150	150	150		150		
Net required quantity			150	300	150	150	450		150		

Figure 6-4. Overall Required Quantity of Part A and Daily Production Plan for Products X and Y

Calculating Lot Composition. There are many cases when production and purchasing cannot be carried out because the quantity of work-in-process and received orders does not equal several times the amount of a fixed quantity. (The same is true regarding certain fixed amounts and loans, even when the company has borrowed capital from a bank.) Such a policy for receiving orders is called a fixed quantity (F/Q) policy. Thus, it is necessary to determine the net quantity for each period as a fixed volume.

This is how we calculate the lot composition. According to the product master plan, a fixed quantity lot size of X is 300 units as determined by the order policy. This will determine the lot composition and be indicated in the daily production plan. In other words, 100 units will be determined for periods 5, 6, and 7 (total = 300) produced in period 5. After that, 100 units will be determined for periods 8, 9, and 10 (total = 300), making the lot composition 300 in period 8.

Calculating Lead Time. We have just seen the lot composition determined at the end of the delivery period. In practice, the calculation must be made by rolling forward only the purchasing lead time portion or the production lead time portion for the first production day of a certain lot, or for the day when an order is received for lot production. Since the parts list specifies that product X's lead time is two periods, in the daily production plan, periods 3 and 6 will be production's start day.

Other Considerations. So far we have explained the basics of calculating required quantities. In practice, however, this process is more complicated than these examples demonstrate. To understand this kind of accounting, it is necessary to understand the policies for receiving orders, after allocation, and spoilage ratio.

First of all, orders are placed for product Y according to the master data and the basic production schedule. This policy, called the master schedule (M/S), is applied to the items on the basic production schedule, which are produced for independent demand. These items represent finished products and, in instances of lagging production or late delivery of goods, it is impossible to satisfy the sales demand even if corresponding products are obtained from

other sources. Consequently, an accounting method that would sub-
tract the amount of remaining inventory and work-in-process is not
used for this type of goods. Furthermore, since final demand products cannot be diverted to other products, it is impossible to create a
lot composition for quantities that are not required. This makes an
accounting of lot composition unnecessary.

Likewise, according to a daily production schedule for product
Y, shown in the upper right table of Figure 6-4, the order policy is to
immediately appropriate the M/S (final demand items, basic production schedule items), remaining inventory (OH), and the net
overall required quantity without subtracting the remaining orders
and WIP (OO).

Next, the quantity required for part A is included in the calculation. The production start date for a product and the number of
orders is evident from the upper part of Figure 6-4. Part A, which is
used for products X and Y, must be completed or delivered on the
day when work on products X and Y begins. The overall required
quantity of part A can be calculated as follows:

Overall required quantity of part A

   (# of product X on day 1) × (# of part A per product X)

   + (# of product Y on day 1) × (# of part A per product Y)

The result of this calculation is indicated in the bottom column
of Figure 6-4. Attention should be paid to the fact that, according to
Figure 6-3's part master data, products X and Y each use one unit of
part A.

Next, the net required quantity of part A is calculated. Table 6-3
uses the terms "already assigned" and "spoilage ratio." "Already
assigned" describes, in this case, a parent part using part A (here, it
is either product X or Y). The inventory that has not yet been
shipped is called "already assigned parts A," describing the status
"on order" (OO). This means that part A has not been shipped and
is still in stock. Consequently, in this case, even if 150 units of products remain in stock (OH), since 80 units have already been assigned, the effective number of inventory units that can be used is 70.

Table 6-3. Planned Required Quantity of Product A and Planned Daily Production

Period	Pre-sent	1	2	3	4	5	6	7	8	9	10
Overall required quantity			150	300	150		450		150		----
After allocation		80									
Spoilage ratio		5	9	18	9		27		9		
Safe number			250								
Required quantity after inclusion		86	409	318	159		477		159		
OH · OO	150	100									
Net required quantity			244	318	159		477		159		
Lot composition			400	200	200		400		200		
Orders on the first day		400	200	200		400		200			

The quantity of already assigned units is included in the calculation of the overall required quantity. The formula is:

Net required quantity

= overall required quantity − (OH + OO − already assigned units)

= overall required quantity + already assigned units) − (OH + OO)

In addition, the already assigned quantity, shown in Table 6-3, is added to period 1 (even though adding to the first day of production for parent parts is theoretically correct).

The spoilage ratio is the estimated ratio when using parent parts (in this case, products X and Y) for child parts (part A). Although this spoilage ratio depends on products X and Y, it is possible to set a single spoilage ratio (6 percent) that is appropriate for the actual demand of part A. Obviously, a different spoilage ratio is necessary for each child part.

According to the part master data of Figure 6-3, the spoilage ratio of part A is 6 percent, while a spoilage ratio of 5 units (80 × 0.06) will be generated for the already assigned quantity of 80 for period 1. A spoilage ratio of 9 units (150 × 0.06) will be generated for the overall required quantity of 150. The same procedure is used for subsequent periods.

A System that Combines MRP and Kanban. As previously mentioned, the use of the kanban method does not necessarily negate the use of MRP. The two are often used jointly. Nonetheless, to what extent must calculating required quantities according to MRP be modified when both methods are used? We will examine the problem by applying the numerical values of Figure 6-4 to Figure 6-5.

A prerequisite for using the kanban method is to standardize production in the final process. Small-lot production is also required for such standardization. As shown in Figure 6-4, the minimum lot sizes for products X and Y are 300 (X) units and 150 (Y) units. In this example, if the minimum lot size for product X is only 20 units, and if production occurs five times daily, it becomes necessary to calculate the lot composition. If the minimum lot size for product Y is 50 units, it still will be necessary to calculate the lot composition.

Since production's lead time is shorter if the lot size is reduced, the lead time portion will have to be rolled forward in the calculation to determine the first day of production. The result is presented in Figure 6-5. The same is true when determining the first day of production for part A and the order quantity.

Even had the kanban method not been used, reducing the production lead time and producing in simultaneous cycles would have attracted attention to the Toyota production system. Japanese companies with multiple processes have employed this method of production since the mid-1970s. One should add that it does not matter whether conditions allowing such a standardization of production included MRP or its joint use with the kanban method. Since there are cases when the kanban method is used to describe the more global Toyota production system, terminology must be used carefully.

Concerning the joint use of MRP and kanban methods, the calculation of required quantities is not the only difference. With MRP, the required quantity is usually calculated weekly, making it possible to employ kanban cards every day for posting weekly production instructions. In other words, the kanban method is used with

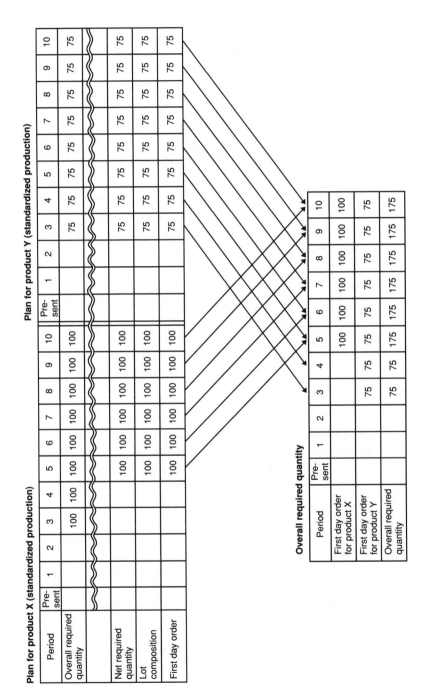

Figure 6-5. Required Quantity for Standardized Production (Leveled Production and Small-Lot Size)

MRP as the means to implement planning. For example, Yamaha engines are manufactured according to the following method.[5]

- Production (or in-process) kanban and receiving kanban are issued according to MRP. This information is sent to the dispatch board in order of priority. This makes it easy to pinpoint delays, to know the order of priority of operations, and so on.
- MRP is used to prepare a macro-plan for parts (to create an order) based on worksite units and to fine-tune the framework of the plan. However, as far as moving things within departments of a worksite is concerned (or dealings between worksites or between manufacturers), the kanban method is used.

MRP Database. The MRP database of production information consists of four master files: two for design technology information and two for production technology information.

Design technology information is composed of the parts master list and the product composition master list. The parts master list has a record of every product, semimanufactured product, part, and raw material. It also notes the following data:

- technological data — part name, unit, drawing number, type code, and material code
- inventory data — storage requirements, remaining stock-on-hand, remaining balance, number of reserves, inventory already assigned, demand total, safe inventory numbers
- order data — order policy, order lots, trade codes
- production data — lead time, order policy, order lots, spoilage ratio, operation-specific codes
- cost data — material demand, labor costs, indirect production costs
- software data — parts list address, process file address, low level code

The product composition master list includes a record of related parts connected by the parent/child parts relationship. For instance, if component parts B and C are manufactured directly for parent part A, one record will register the A/B relationship and another will register the A/C relationship. In this way, the following data are recorded:

1. The *parent part address* records the number of the parts master that shows a corresponding parent part.
2. The *child part address* records the number of the parts master that shows a corresponding child part.
3. The *part number* indicates which unit part is required for each unit of the parent part.
4. The *supply code* indicates whether or not compensation is required for child parts (if they are manufactured by external subcontractors).
5. The *software data* consists of all parts master lists and addresses.

Production technology information refers to the process master list and the operation-specific master list. The process master list contains a record of every process that each product or part undergoes. For example, if part A goes through three processes, there are three records relating to part A. Each record lists the following data:

• process name
• number of the specific operation segment
• process time
• standard process time for each piece
• number of workers required

The operations segment master list contains a record for each operation segment and a corresponding record that lists the following data:

• name of the operation segment
• department affiliation number
• ratio of labor costs and a ratio of indirect production
• average transportation time
• time of possible employment

The production information database containing the four master files just described usually is maintained and updated by a production information manager.

Cost Accounting Systems Based on MRP Database. Production control methods based on MRP use different production number methods. In addition, the production number of the parent part is not always attributed to each part on the order sheet. For this reason, product cost accounting based on MRP uses multistage parts lists in which calculations can be done by adding up sums in order, starting from the bottom and continuing upward. For example, once the cost of the grandchild part is computed, the child part is calculated and added to this cost. On top of that is added the cost of the parent part.

The merit of similar cost accumulating systems based on multistage parts composition is that they enable one to calculate a product's standard cost as well as its latest cost. It is simple to calculate the latest cost, and if at some stage the material demand for a part changes, this system permits changing only the materials cost for this part by computer processing.

Traditional standard cost accounting methods employ standard costs that remain constant throughout the accounting period. This leads to a number of problems. The advantages of the new cost accounting systems, however, lie in their ability to overcome these problems. These advantages can be described as follows:

1. Because the production department determines sales prices, profit and loss figures on product orders already received can be based on the most recent costs.

2. Because the production department can operate with profit margins based on the latest costs, it is possible to formulate a sales strategy using an optimal product mix and similar strategic aspects.

3. During the product development stage, the standard costs set at the design stage are arrived at by incorporating the costs that must be met by the design, technology, purchasing, and manufacturing departments. In each case it is possible to quickly present design changes, changes caused by value engineering (VE) and new equipment, changes caused by internal and external operations, and other changes relevant to the most recent cost estimate.

4. The monthly settlement of accounts and other calculations required for standard costs can be handled promptly.
5. The new cost accounting methods are useful in controlling costs. Because standard costs are usually frozen for the period of one accounting year, the difference between these standard costs and real costs is calculated as the variable cost. Standard costs can use this as a control target. When variances between standard costs and the most recent costs reflect current fluctuations, greater cost control over parts is possible.

We will now examine the importance of a MRP database and how to apply it to the new cost accounting systems.

Building Up Costs from Low Level Codes. Databases that serve to build up the structure of standard costs and the most recent costs use a parts master and a product composition table (or parts list) describing a product's or part's direct material costs and processing costs related to outside production. A process master is used for direct labor costs while an operation segment master is used for indirect production costs.

A cost buildup starts with the part at the lowest position on the parts sheet and continues through each higher level. In a multistage parts sheet, illustrated in Figure 6-6, low level codes (LLC) are used

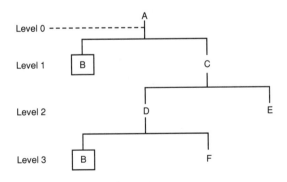

Figure 6-6. Low Level Code (LLC) of Part B

so that part B's unit price is calculated only once even though this same part B may be used in multiple stages.

Labor Costs and Plant Overhead. A work center master file includes data on labor costs and factory overhead. A process master file contains standard operation time per process and information on the code numbers of the work center where each process belongs. Therefore, the labor and overhead costs of part B during processing would be calculated as follows:

$$\text{Labor costs} = \sum_{i=1}^{n} (\text{Standard time} \times \text{wage ratio of operation segment})$$

$$\text{Indirect costs} = \sum_{i=1}^{n} (\text{Standard time} \times \text{ratio of indirect costs of operation segment})$$

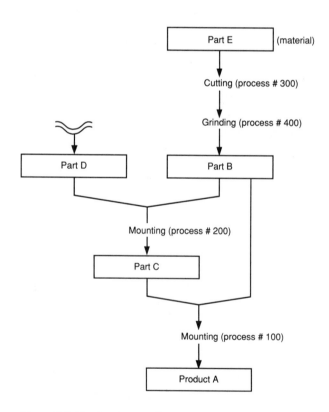

Figure 6-7. The Production Flow of Product A

Examples of Product Cost Accounting. Figure 6-7 shows the flow of production processes for product A. The material required for part E is steel. Part B is obtained after treatment by the cutting and grinding process. Part D is also finished on the plant floor, although with fewer processing operations. Part C is assembled from parts B and D. Finally, product A is completed by assembling parts C and B.

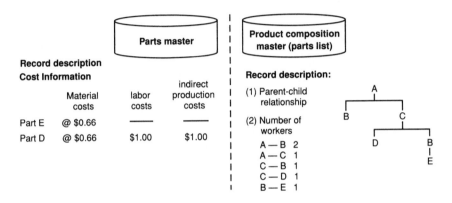

Figure 6-8. Information on Design Technology

Figure 6-8 conveys information on design technology in terms of the cost data and the composition of parts (product tree). The material costs, labor costs, and plant overhead of part D have been calculated.

Figure 6-9 shows processing data related to plant floor processing of part B and the assembly of parts A and C.

Based on the database presented in Figures 6-8 and 6-9, it is possible to calculate the cost of product A. The results are shown in Table 6-4 in the form of a cost accounting table.

Standard Costs and Accounting Tables for the Latest Costs. When part numbers are fed into a computer, material costs, labor costs, indirect production costs of standard costs, and the latest cost of all the parts found one level below this part number are displayed on a single level parts list (see Figure 6-10).

Part number	Process number	Process description	Standard time	Operation segment number	Operation segment number	Wage ratio	Indirect cost ratio
A	100	Mounting of parts B and C	2 HR	101	101	50	70
					201	100	180
C	200	Mounting of parts B and D	1 HR	201	202	90	200
B	300	Cutting	1 HR	202			
	400	Grinding	0.5 HR	202			

Process master   **Operation segment master**

Record description:

Figure 6-9. Production and Technology Information

Table 6-4. The Cost Accounting Process for Individual Products

Product number	Item	Material costs	Labor costs	Indirect production costs	Total
Product E	Total	$0.66	$	$	$0.66
Part B	Part D	100	—	—	100
	Process 300		90	200	290
	Process 400		45	100	145
	Total	100	135	300	535
Part D	Total	100	150	150	400
Part C	Part B	100	135	300	535
	Part D	100	150	150	400
	Process 200		100	180	280
	Total	200	385	630	1,215
Product A	Part C	200	385	630	1,215
	Part B	200	270	600	1,070
	Process 100		100	140	240
	Total	400	755	1,370	2,525

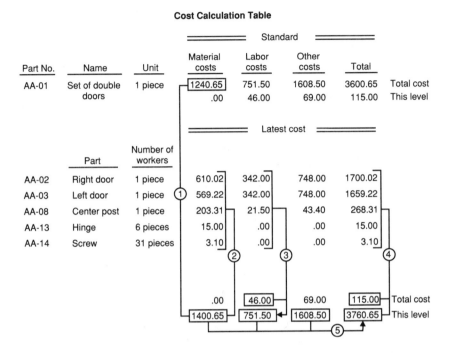

Cost Calculation Table

=== Standard ===

Part No.	Name	Unit	Material costs	Labor costs	Other costs	Total	
AA-01	Set of double doors	1 piece	1240.65	751.50	1608.50	3600.65	Total cost
			.00	46.00	69.00	115.00	This level

=== Latest cost ===

	Part	Number of workers					
AA-02	Right door	1 piece	610.02	342.00	748.00	1700.02	
AA-03	Left door	1 piece	569.22	342.00	748.00	1659.22	
AA-08	Center post	1 piece	203.31	21.50	43.40	268.31	
AA-13	Hinge	6 pieces	15.00	.00	.00	15.00	
AA-14	Screw	31 pieces	3.10	.00	.00	3.10	

	.00	46.00	69.00	115.00	Total cost
	1400.65	751.50	1608.50	3760.65	This level

Figure 6-10. Comparison Table of Standard Costs and Latest Costs

Figure 6-10 shows a difference of $1.00 between the standard cost and the latest material cost. This means that the material costs of parts that compose the latest cost figures have risen $1.00 since the standard cost was determined.

The cost accounting list also shows added costs divided into individual costs per level and accumulated (or total) costs. In this example, there are five child parts (right door, left door, center post, hinge, screw) that are mounted into a set of double doors. Since the processing cost of this mounting operation are on the same level, however, the costs of the five child parts are added together to create the level cost. This is the total cost of the part (the set of double doors).

7

Profit and Cost Management at Kubota: A Divisional Control System

In this chapter, we will examine cases illustrating profit management and cost management methods at Kubota Company, Ltd. As a manufacturer of tractors, in a broad sense Kubota belongs to the automobile manufacturing industry.

In 1978, a surplus of rice in Japan forced the government to initiate a second program to reduce rice production. As a result, there was a tendency toward farming in dry fields as opposed to traditional rice paddy cultivation. Under these conditions, the production of tractors was diversified to meet the demands of farmers.

As the market for tractors grew, so did rivalry among manufacturers in Japan. To compensate for this intense competition, there was strong impetus to expand and diversify product lines destined for foreign markets. With the increasing appreciation of the yen, however, export figures declined. Also, as regulations on the import of farm products were liberalized, negative aspects arose, such as demands for a more liberal policy regarding rice production. In turn there arose a "differentiation strategy" with the purpose of adding new capabilities to products and creating a more diversified product line that could be differentiated easily from its competitors.

An emphasis on wide-variety small-lot production emerged in the industry's manufacturing systems. At Kubota, traditional accounting control systems focused on profit control and cost improvements. Under these circumstances, the importance of awareness in the profit share of individual products increased. In order to increase awareness of the product differentiation strategy, revolutionary structural changes were implemented.

In April 1984, I began to examine (1) the structural organization of the internal combustion engine division at Kubota's Tsukuba plant, (2) the structure of previous function differentiation (sales headquarters, production headquarters, research headquarters, and so forth), and (3) changes in product diversification.

This chapter will concentrate on profit control (and profit awareness) of individual products in internal company divisions rather than in plant units. While in a plant many company divisions produce a great number of individual products, we will focus on concrete examples illustrating profit control and cost control and actual circumstances at the Tsukuba plant where tractors for agricultural use are manufactured.

The author expresses his appreciation to Yoshiaki Okada, chief of the Tsukuba plant's control section, and to Yuji Yamaguchi, chief of the cost down (CD) promotion section at the same plant, for their invaluable assistance.

The Relationship between the Head Office, Operation Headquarters, Operation Divisions, and Plant and Management Functions. Kubota's current structural organization can be summarized as follows. Departments responsible for management and organization are those divisions that conduct management activities within the entire company, starting with the staff of the company president at the head office. Formerly, management divisions were divided into control divisions and management divisions for external reporting. Then both divisions merged, giving the management division control over several operation headquarters.

General control divisions, responsible for control and management tasks, are located at each operations headquarters. Within operations headquarters, several divisions are responsible for individual products. Consequently, operations headquarters control several operations divisions and perform a wide range of small business unit (SBU) functions. Finally, within each operations division is a planning division that is responsible for controlling respective operations departments.

Briefly, Kubota's operations divisions are:

1. internal combustion engine operations headquarters
2. pipe operations headquarters
3. mechanical operations headquarters
4. building materials and equipment operations headquarters
5. environment facilities operations headquarters
6. material operations division

Selecting the headquarters for mechanical operations, for example, we will find that it consists of the following operations divisions:

- pump operations division
- valve operations division
- automatic vending machine operations division
- electrical transmission devices operations division
- grinding machine operations division
- overseas engineering operations division

In clarifying the relationship between the operations divisions and the plants, it is rare to have a relationship in which one operations division corresponds to one plant. There are, however, many cases of several operations divisions coexisting within one plant. Conversely, there are also many cases when one operations division is responsible for a number of plants.

Similar relationships are not limited to Kubota. In recent years, they can be observed in other Japanese companies. For instance, although Toyota's Tsukuba plant belongs to the internal combustion engine operations headquarters, within the plant we will see tractor operations, engine operations, parts operations, and other divisions. There are also sales divisions and technology divisions of several plants within each division.

Every plant is managed by a control department, which is responsible for accounting, cost accounting, and other functions that ensure the profitability of each division. These are managed jointly through profit centers.

The department for cost down (CD) promotion in the plant, the production control department, and other departments provide joint control over several operations divisions located within the plant. For instance, the department for production control jointly manages each division within a certain plant because of the mechanization and automatization of parts manufacturing. This represents the output of each operations division for the manufacture of parts. Also, parts made by the engine operations division and used in engine assembly lines, products made by the tractor operations divisions and used in tractor assembly lines, as well as other products are placed on conveyors in a certain order because each component forms a part of a circulating flow of parts and products.

The Relationship between Profit Control Systems and Cost Control Systems. A profit control system allows the comparative variance analysis of planned monthly profit figures and actual profit. This analysis is based on organizational units at each organizational stage according to a target control system that breaks down profit targets from top to bottom.

First, the profit target is set by the company president for the entire company. This target is then broken down into profit targets assigned to six operations divisions. In addition, the profit target of a specific operations headquarters is divided among the operations divisions of that operations headquarters. Next, the profit target of each operations division is divided into profit targets for individual products produced or used in the operations division. All the profit targets of individual products manufactured in every plant division are then added up to arrive at the overall profit target of the plant.

At Kubota's Tsukuba plant, individual products are divided into twenty-two classes: eight classes of products in the tractor operations division, ten classes in the engineering operations division, and four classes in the parts operations division.

Since 1988 when the revolutionary changes in the structure of operations systems took place at Kubota, control over the profitability of individual products has been tightened. Although profit variance analysis is conducted monthly for each product in every division of the plant, it is company policy to conduct cost variance analysis as part of the profit variance analysis. Variance analysis and expense item variance analysis is also done for costs in each production area. With the aid of computers, the time required for variance analysis is less than fifteen days. Information reflecting calculated variance is distributed at departmental meetings.

Consequently, the primary aim of the plant's financial controls (on which its managerial accounting system is based) is profit control over each product and each division and cost controls in individual production areas and over individual expense items. In addition, control is based on data that measures the amount of material used to evaluate productivity, the inventory of work-in-process and material in stock, and similar factors. Control over the actual quantities produced is enforced by applying standard numbers to basic units of expense items in each production area. This represents one of the main pillars of the organization of divisions.

The problem at present is how to interpret quantitative data on a daily and weekly "visual control" basis since the variance information, as described, is not gathered through direct on-site control. In this respect, we could say that variance information fulfills the function of a check conducted on a managerial level, a level higher than on-the-spot control.

Performance Evaluation in Divisions. We will now look at the characteristics of performance evaluation in divisions and how they relate to profit control. To evaluate divisions, Kubota uses four criteria:

1. profit
2. development
3. quality
4. business results in money received

Profit is determined by comparing the real profit of the present period to that of the previous period. The reason a comparison is not made with the profit target for the present period is that a target does not necessarily reflect environmental conditions with accuracy.

Furthermore, numbers reflecting the rate of return on capital invested (ROI) in the operations division is also evaluated. This ROI element expresses recurring profit. The fact that such emphasis is placed on comparing the profit from the previous period while no comparison is made to the profit target probably reflects a consideration for evaluating the business performance of the overall plant. On the other hand, to stimulate the conscientious control and improvement of profit in operations divisions, it is necessary to utilize numbers reflecting the profit variance analysis. Finally, figures reflecting a sales profit ratio are often calculated for each operations division or group.

Quality includes, among other things, the number of customer complaints.

Business results in money received are business results derived from evaluations of: (1) profit and loss in terms of commercial profitability (based on business performance in operations divisions), (2) new product development, and (3) guarantees of quality. A comprehensive evaluation of financial (and other) business results in money received is also conducted.

Cost Accounting Methods. The form of cost accounting used at the Tsukuba plant is the *seiban* cost accounting method. In this method, seiban are numerical codes on a production diagram on which individual orders are entered. These seiban numbers not only indicate a final product, but are linked to indices of shipped parts, grandchild parts, and great-grandchild parts. For instance, when doing cost accounting for each operations division, both grandchild parts and child parts are integrated in the calculation. Final product costs can be calculated from child parts because calculations are based on the sequential numbers of the production diagram.

Databases containing cost units of standard cost systems also use MRP databases for production control. This means the joint use of parts list (bill of material) data. However, since cost accounting is not carried out for individual parts apart from the respective steps on each level of the part composition table, we could say that accounting according to the individual seiban numbers of a final product is a traditional accounting method.

Based on direct cost accounting standards, direct labor costs are considered to be variable costs. Accordingly, monthly fixed costs are regulated so as to calculate the recurring profit from the total cost accounting standard. The distribution of indirect production costs in the plants is carried out according to production quantities per standard number of workers. This represents the primary indirect costs in each production area. (An exception is the machining area where this distribution is based on the number of machine hours.) The general categories of joint costs are:

1. joint costs of operation headquarters and expenses other than those of operations divisions
2. joint costs for each department of an operations division
3. a plant's indirect production costs

These costs are allocated as two halves of one item of expenditure. Fifty percent is proportional to the amount of goods shipped from individual groups (individual products) of operations divisions. The other 50 percent is allocated in proportion to the number of workers (or labor hours). These operational characteristics are considered to be very important.

In March 1988 at its main office, Kubota introduced as a secondary accounting system an accounting control information system called the Advanced Accounting Management System (ADAMS). This system uses IBM Japan's software with built-in MATPLAN designed to assist cost accounting and the decision-making process. MATPLAN is an interactive software program based on the structured matrix approach. The cost accounting system used at the plants is based on ADAMS.

As far as accounting for plant and equipment investment are concerned, both the rate of return on investment and the net recovery period method are used. It is often advisable to introduce plant and equipment investment management earlier than planned to ensure the manufacture of quality products.

Cost Planning. When the operations division system was adopted, cost planning functions were centralized in the planning divisions of every operations division connected with internal combustion engines. Although these planning divisions are located at company headquarters, the technology division is located in the Sakai plant.

The plants are participating more and more in cost planning activities that are conducted in parallel. These activities primarily concern three issues:

1. Since the relationship between principal cooperating manufacturers is based on trust, target costs and specifications regarding parts and unit products are shared on the basis of contracts. In addition, parts are designed to meet target costs and specifications. Since cost planning refers to specifications for new models, however, there is the possibility of secrets being leaked to rival companies. In this respect, trust limitations do exist among cooperating manufacturers.
2. When equipment investment is required for new models, plants initially will present a proposal that is compatible with the design and equipment concept.
3. Reducing the number of parts influences productivity. In other words, it becomes possible to attain the advantages of mass production by reducing the number of parts.

These activities permit the creation of a simultaneous multistage design. This design is based on the concept of group technology (GT) and incorporates a design of parts that satisfies requirements from various orders. This is done to include all necessary specifications from the beginning and to eliminate any consequent changes.

To give an example, the following actions are taken to produce a processing line for engines with varying numbers of cylinders. Equipment capable of accommodating the largest four-cylinder engine is put in position first. The cutting equipment is then arranged sequentially for one less cylinder. This eliminates the need for significant plan changes, and it is possible to manufacture engines ranging in capacity from 15 to 45 horsepower, even if the cylinder's diameter is increased or reduced or the number of revolutions is changed.

Similarly, a tractor transmission case was designed for combined use. Since it is possible to change the thickness of the casing and increase the number of ports depending on the engine's horsepower, the design was adjusted to accommodate changes of the port diameter. Thus, when the wheel base is changed, it is possible to increase or decrease the length of the inserted area, which is called mid-case. These changes were integrated with three types of sheet metal.

As a result of design and productivity strategies aimed at emulating the advantages of mass production, it became possible to introduce large standard automated machines commonly used by auto makers. A merit of this equipment is that it has six lines for producing the main parts of transfer machines. It also permits the use of automatic assembly machines.

In other plants, the following measures are applied to cost planning. Problems encountered in the course of trial manufacturing are studied plantwide and innovative proposals requested. Technical service is examined. The technology and service division is located next to the Tsukuba plant.

The period required for cost planning is approximately three years, a necessary time frame in case of model changes. In the first year, concepts for new models are determined in meetings held with marketing people. During the next seven to ten months, they prepare for production. The following year sees the design concept of a new model developed further, a target cost assigned to it, and details worked out regarding design and cost requirements.

Three years might be considered a long period for cost planning until we realize that the life cycle of a tractor with a full model engine is six to seven years, during which one or two minor engines are also developed.

8

Profit Management and Cost Management in the Responsibility Accounting System

How are cost accounting and profit management systems being used in the Japanese auto industry's production and sales environments? This chapter looks at how a prominent Japanese auto maker, who at the company's request will be referred to as Company X, is adapting the new cost management methods to its own set of circumstances.

How Auto Makers Distinguish Types of Costs. The most important cost elements in the auto industry are direct material costs and processing costs. Processing costs can be divided further into indirect material costs, labor costs, and indirect management costs as shown in Figure 8-1.

We can divide production costs into direct material costs, direct management costs, direct labor costs, direct fixed costs, development costs, and common costs. For management purposes, these costs can then be categorized into proportional costs and fixed costs, or direct costs and common costs as shown in Figure 8-2.

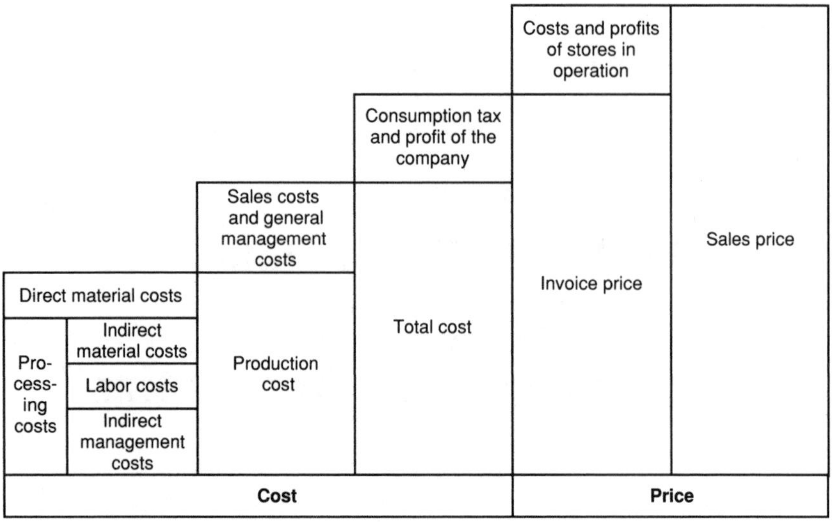

			Costs and profits of stores in operation	
		Consumption tax and profit of the company		
	Sales costs and general management costs			Sales price
Direct material costs			Invoice price	
Pro-cess-ing costs	Indirect material costs	Production cost	Total cost	
	Labor costs			
	Indirect management costs			
Cost			**Price**	

Figure 8-1. An Itemized Structure of Automobile Costs

Rough percentages making up the total cost composition of Japanese auto makers begin with direct material costs, which account for approximately 70 percent of the total cost. In other words, items purchased from outside vendors represent 70 percent of the cost. The remaining 30 percent includes amortization and labor costs. Proportional costs represent 80 percent and fixed costs

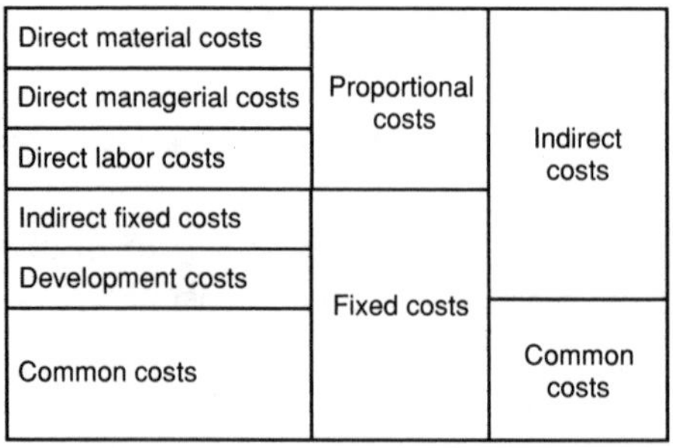

Direct material costs	Proportional costs	Indirect costs
Direct managerial costs		
Direct labor costs		
Indirect fixed costs	Fixed costs	
Development costs		
Common costs		Common costs

Production costs are subdivided not on financial accounting purposes but on management accounting purposes (proportional costs, fixed costs, direct costs, common costs).

Figure 8-2. Types of Production Costs

represent 20 percent of the total. This is because direct material costs make up 70 percent of production costs.

Since direct costs can be traced directly to a specific product, 90 percent of direct costs are material costs. In this context, specific product refers to products used in specific car types. These products represent 90 percent of the total cost and common management costs represent the remaining 10 percent. How proportional costs, fixed costs, direct costs, and common costs are used will be explained later.

One problem is that direct labor costs are treated as proportional costs. While direct labor costs represent a percentage of costs that grows as production increases, when production flattens or decreases, they become difficult to reduce. Nevertheless, there is a great deal of support and cooperation among individual plants and departments in the automobile industry, and they can regard direct labor costs as proportional as long as they are able to absorb the surplus labor in different departments.

Figure 8-2 has a column for direct fixed costs. Primarily, direct fixed costs refer to the amortization of equipment, maintenance costs, insurance premiums, and similar costs. The proportion of these costs is high. With automation, the proportion of costs connected with production and assembly lines has risen. While it became possible to gradually reduce labor costs, direct fixed costs increased. A decade ago, the majority of assembly line costs was direct labor costs. With the percentage of direct fixed costs on the rise, this is no longer true.

In any case, they could allocate direct fixed costs to individual car types. It was possible to allocate equipment costs incurred exclusively for car A or exclusively for car B. Incidentally, in view of the increasing rationalization and standardization of equipment, this type of direct allocation becomes more difficult. As equipment standardization progresses, it will no longer be necessary to use specialized equipment for car A. The same equipment will be used for cars B or C. Consequently, while the volume of direct fixed costs for individual cars has risen over time, from a cost accounting perspective, the percentage of direct fixed costs remains relatively low. This is due to the joint use of equipment and standardized parts.

The bulk of development funds goes to research and development for direct allocation to individual car types. Operating costs, advertising costs, supplementary costs, transportation costs and so on are also allocated to individual car types. We will discuss later how the results of these allocations are used.

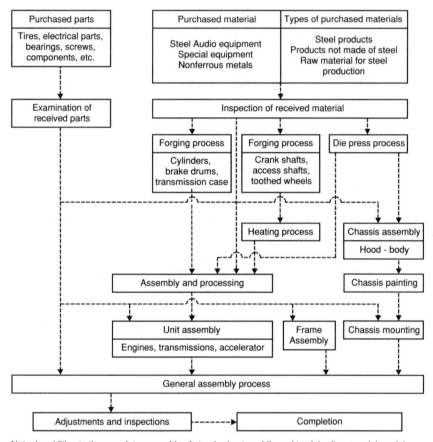

Note: In addition to the complete assembly of standard automobile and truck bodies, special model chassis are also assembled, with the exception of some parts.

Figure 8-3. The Process of Automobile and Parts Production

Cost Accounting Methods. Until now, cost accounting in the Japanese auto industry was done according to the textbook. It could be said, in fact, that there was only one model.

Standard Cost Accounting. The goal of standard cost accounting is to simplify the calculation of real product costs according to a standard textbook model. Here we will examine how some companies deal with standard cost accounting.

Certain companies are characterized by such control that standard costs have become real standard costs. Costs are set for every part for a period of one year. Cars typically contain 1,000 to 2,000 types of parts per type, each car body using between 50,000 and 60,000 such parts. Every one of them must be reviewed to determine their estimated standard cost for the one-year period. Although computers are used for these calculations, managing all of the car types with their various parts requires the use of standard costs. These standard costs are determined yearly by the accounting department.

These standard costs are also used in the area of responsibility accounting, which will be described later, as a standard for setting transfer prices. At some point, these standard costs are used to create yearly specifications and cost level effectiveness; for instance, applying 1990 specifications to March. In financial accounting, on the other hand, cost management is based on cost variables. Still, standard costs are used in financial accounting to evaluate inventory assets at the end of a period and to adjust cost variables.

Figure 8-3 illustrates the cost system for a plant's individual processes. Process-specific operation cost systems are used for respective processes, such as assembling units at various assembly plants and the subassembly of materials, raw material, and parts purchased from outside vendors. The production costs for one process become the material costs of the next process.

Actual Cost Accounting. Actual cost accounting is carried out in three steps: incurred costs are broken down (1) by individual cost element, (2) by individual cost center, and (3) by individual product costs. This breakdown is shown in Figure 8-4.

First, individual cost elements are broken down into cost accounting elements that are used to interpret the budget by comparing the costs of individual processes. A single process can be quite long, and while it might be difficult to break it down into smaller segments, it can be divided roughly into painting, assembly, body processing, and similar elements. (Refer to Figure 8-3's overview of individual process elements in the manufacturing process.)

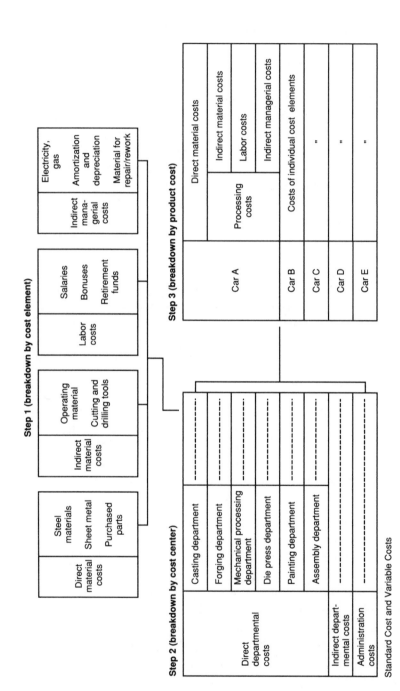

Figure 8-4. Three Steps of Actual Cost Accounting for Automobile Production

If the system is to make sense, the most important material costs must be examined on the basis of individual processing machines. Besides the customary cost accounting systems, there are methods that combine cost elements according to machine. With the push toward more detailed cost control methods, recent management trends are characterized by a gradual expansion of the range of cost elements dealt with on this basis.

Consequently, considering that a primary task in body welding plants is robotization, accounting by individual cost elements is also important if we want to know the energy consumption per machine and per robot, maintenance costs (including the cost of replacing parts), the waiting time, and the defect ratio. When such detailed objectives are not required, however, the task will be to deal only with one cost element, for instance the pressing process, the body process, assembly process, and so on.

The second step of actual cost accounting involves calculating the cost elements in the individual cost centers.

The third step involves the costs of individual products or commodities, for instance, of car types A, B, C, and so forth. In other words, this step establishes the cost of a single car A or a single car B. This is actual cost accounting's most important aim — to provide the cost of individual products. This step also allows us to calculate income for each car type.

Nevertheless, even in a single class category for car A, there will be big differences between a deluxe model selling for $36,000 and a popular model selling for $13,000. This means that there will also be a big difference between the price-earning ratios of the two cars. If we create a line of car A with as many as 1,000 models, there is no way to establish the variable costs within that line. Using the actual cost accounting method, however, we can break down the costs into small units. It is possible, for instance, to divide the car A group into cars with engine capacities of 2,000 or 3,000 cubic centimeters.

This data is important when formulating marketing strategies. In fact, it is perhaps the most important information used by the accounting department because, to formulate its sales strategies, the sales department needs to know the exact amount of projected income and costs. The sales department must receive this information as quickly as possible.

There are process planning methods that allocate a product's processing costs (excluding material costs). We must know the number of workers in each process for every car model. To arrive at the distribution ratio of processing costs, the amount of processing costs per process is divided by the number of direct labor hours (or minutes). Consequently, the direct labor hour rate is still being used. To understand the cost of parts, we first must create a standard for the distribution of processing costs. The standard is based on direct labor hours divided by the processing costs generated in each process. (This is because Company X does not base its allocation calculation on the standard distribution of machine hours.)

Variable Cost Accounting. As explained in connection with standard costs, the difference between the standard cost and the actual cost is the variable production cost. Standard cost refers to costs at a given point at the beginning or end of a period in a fiscal year. Subsequent fluctuations of standard costs are called variable costs. In this instance, this variance is a large sum because Company X uses the broad categories of "cost reduction variable" and "management variable."

The cost reduction variable is used by many companies. This is due to the recent appreciation of the yen, which makes it possible to reduce the cost of purchased goods. Together with this cost reduction, we have witnessed variable costs on a large scale. Purchased goods as well as increased productivity within a company are contributing factors to the cost reduction achieved during the course of a year. An increase in material reserves is usually encouraged in the form of variable budget costs. In the case of processing costs, cost reduction is usually encouraged in the form of variable efficiency costs.

Management variables reflect real costs as precisely as possible because automobile specifications change from day to day. It requires a lot of time-consuming work to be able to deal with accurate actual costs.

For example, by the end of March 1990, when the standard of initial specifications was prepared, a large management variable (specifications variable) was created in the form of a budget variable. In any case, actual costs are presented with enough cost variables to make up the difference between the standard cost and the production cost variable. Also, to understand the precise production cost of different car types using cost accounting by product, it is important to understand how these cost variables are reflected in each car type.

Finally, we should also mention that although the sales department would like detailed cost descriptions of individual products, the accounting department cannot always make this detailed information available, because it can cover as much as 1,000 types of cars. (We saw in Chapter 1, however, that Toyota includes all of this information in its calculations.)

How this cost information should be presented is often a bone of contention between the accounting and sales departments. With 1,000 versions of car A, there will be some 100,000 overall design specifications. For calculations of this magnitude, the accounting department needs computers and a large staff.

Job Order Cost Accounting. No Japanese auto maker is using job order cost accounting to a significant degree. On the other hand, manufacturers working within the framework of a diversified company use job order cost accounting for tackling individual orders of large projects, such as a spaceship or textile machinery.

Estimated Cost Accounting. Estimated cost accounting is used for the cost control of new automobiles. For companies belonging to the Toyota group, this is part of a cost planning process during which estimates of part costs are made.

Company X takes approximately three and a half years before most of its automobiles are ready for sales. This period covers the moment when the first blueprint sketches are drawn to when the car is delivered to the customer. During this time, one-third of the models have fixed costs; for the remaining two-thirds, cost control is about to begin.

There are several two- and three-step monitoring systems for cost control. In the end, a cost estimate will be needed to determine the sales price. A main concern of the accounting department is determining that final cost estimate. Earlier in the monitoring process, individual departments were responsible for individual costs.

Estimated cost accounting differs from real cost accounting in that one has to wait several years to find out the cost of the special equipment needed to produce a new car, or to find out the development cost of a special model. In view of these problems, determining the payback and amortization periods is imperative.

The typical life span of an automobile has been shortened considerably. It is referred to as "replacement with a new car." In the past, a new car model would last about four years, a time period that, despite minor fluctuations, was fairly constant. Recently, however, it seems that, even though there may be a great deal of attention generated by introducing a new car, after two years, no one will remember it — and a new car will be unveiled. This is normal today.

Consequently, since the payback period for special costs is not yet determined, it is difficult to tell when the costs will be recovered. The result under these circumstances is that the waiting period for return of costs differs with each model.

In any event, if it is necessary to estimate the cost of 2,000 parts, the estimate must be broken down into cost estimates for 2,000 elements of 2,000 parts, the reason being that 70 percent of an automobile consists of component parts purchased from outside suppliers. Thus, an important factor in determining the possibility of cost reduction is to enter as early as possible into cost arrangements with cooperating manufacturers.

Accordingly, it is important for a company to present concrete specifications, quality standards, and similar requirements to other manufacturers early on in the three-and-a-half-year period. This requires concrete specifications for even the smallest part. The timely procurement of estimated costs for every part at this stage is a critical feature in this accounting process.

Actual Cost Accounting by Car. Actual cost accounting by car presents the actual cost of individual parts. By following the steps of estimated cost accounting, it is possible to estimate the cost of manufacturing a particular car or to estimate the planned costs (Toyota's target cost). Once these costs are established, however, it must be ascertained that they have been met. The resulting accounting procedure is called "actual cost accounting by car." While every part should undergo this process, because of the time involved, actual cost estimates are applied to representative parts only.

For Company X, determining actual costs of each part of every car is important because this reveals whether or not it will be possible to maintain the cost of the car as calculated during the planning stage. When the life span of an automobile was four years, even though costs were subject to market fluctuations, knowing in advance whether Company X would be able to meet the planned (or target) cost was important to both the production and cost planning departments.

The Responsibility Accounting System. The goal of responsibility accounting, in particular those systems that emphasize the profit responsibility of accounting, is to inculcate the concept of profit in every department. This is one reason why the responsibility accounting system was introduced by Company X.

With the possible exception of some U.S. companies, the usual organizational form of a company in the auto industry is divisional — meaning that profit-and-loss accounting is the responsibility of the individual departments. However, it is difficult to implement a system based on divisional organization due to the complexity of the distribution and transfer of products and parts between departments. Because parts and products are transferred many times, it is difficult to set corresponding internal transfer prices.

Japanese auto makers have adopted an organizational system where administrative power is centralized. This permits the distribution of different functions to different departments. Implementing a new system must be difficult from the standpoint of divisional organization. Although it did not radically change its organizational structure beforehand, Company X introduced the profit responsibility accounting system. This permitted a greater flow of information and products companywide and conveyed the concept of costs as well as profit to every department.

Responsibility Accounting by Department and Product. The difficult task of a system that is based on responsibility accounting is defining both the extent of responsibilities and the internal transfer prices. Within a plant, the plant manager is responsible for providing costs to the plant's cost center. This role of the plant manager must be considered within the scope of overall responsibilities.

Because 70 percent of a car's cost is material costs and 30 percent is processing costs, most purchases are handled through a central purchasing system. This allows the purchasing department to control prices to some extent, while the design department determines design specifications and other departments make other decisions. A plant manager's decision-making responsibilities regarding cost control are, therefore, limited. At Company X, the problem of involving employees more actively in cost reduction activities is crucial. The number of workers in one plant alone grew from 3,000 to 4,000 with salaries and hourly wages reaching $333 million. In the end, to reduce its costs a company must reduce (1) the defective product waste in every department of the plant, (2) the number of workers, or (3) the amount of purchased parts. This makes motivating employees to achieve these reductions a major responsibility of the plant manager.

Textbooks point out that responsibility accounting systems consist of two building blocks:

- responsibility accounting by individual department
- responsibility accounting by individual product

Responsibility accounting by individual departments can be viewed as a vertical axis forming a continuous line of job-specific functions in each department within a plant — operations or sales, for example.

In contrast, responsibility accounting based on a single car means that for a certain level of cost the plant must achieve a certain level of profit. This can be regarded as the horizontal axis of responsibility accounting. In other words, car A is developed and produced so that the sales people, who are all connected by the horizontal axis of responsibility accounting, will know how much profit must be realized on this type of car. Within this system, a "responsibility unit" represents every product. These units include designers working on new product development as well as sales people.

Profit Improvement: The Role of Contribution Profit in Achieving Improved Costs. The concept of contribution profit arose from the linking of individual products with responsibility accounting systems. The concept of responsibility profit is necessary

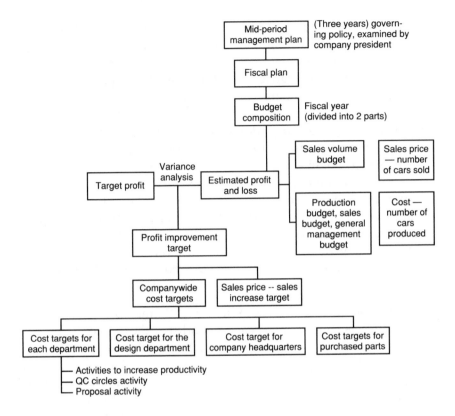

Figure 8-5. Profit Planning and Cost Reduction Activities

because a plant does not produce just one type of car — it produces several at a time. Therefore, besides the plant manager, different managers are responsible for the various products. These product managers are the responsible people on the horizontal axis.

For example, when the output rate for car A is affected by stagnating sales in the United States, it becomes impossible to recover the plant's fixed costs. This, in turn, will have a negative repercussion on the plant's production of cars B and C. Thus, it is only natural that managers responsible for individual products have some responsibility for other products as well.

To avoid this situation, Company X adopted the contribution profit system. Accordingly, cost control over individual products is exercised on the basis of the profit from previous contributions rather than by subtracting fixed costs from the profit. As shown in Figure 8-5, which explains profit planning and cost reduction activities, an intermediate management business plan is prepared for the period in order to prepare business plans for each fiscal year. (An intermediate business plan is prepared every three years.) This makes it possible to break down cost targets and target profits by department and product for each budget period.

It is then possible to compare actual costs and actual profits. In particular, one can create profit improvement targets by conducting a variance analysis of estimated profit and loss and of target profits. One profit improvement target is a cost target applied company-wide. Other targets represent sales cost targets and targeted increases in the number of cars sold. This is how profit improvements are actually achieved. The responsibility accounting system assumes that profit management is a main support of the cost structure.

Internal Transfer Prices. When considering how to set internal transfer prices, one should bear in mind that these prices represent the most essential component of the responsibility system. A price-setting method frequently discussed in textbooks is applying transfer prices that are based on market standards — market prices of actual products. There are also many cases of products not on the market that will be classified at some point with standard prices (although without additional profit) for purposes of the internal transfer of prices. During the first fiscal year of production of a specific car model, it is possible to determine that the target price, which represents the planned sales price, will be used as the transfer price.

Problems Facing the Industry. One can expect plant changes in the auto industry to continue. Simplified and industrywide characteristics of equipment and rational production methods are indispensable components of these changes. Another tendency that will be emphasized in the future is product diversification. Thus, the accounting department's task is to discover how to apply cost management systems and cost accounting within the framework of a more universal and multipurpose employment of the industry's equipment and future product diversification.

In view of the growing trend toward production of parts and products overseas, another problem facing the auto industry is how to consolidate the cost accounting systems of these overseas companies and plants. Although their traditional cost accounting systems differ, companies wishing to cooperate successfully overseas must find ways to consolidate international accounting methods.

9

Full Cost-based Transfer Pricing in the Japanese Auto Industry: Risk-sharing and Risk-spreading Behavior* **

This chapter describes the risk-sharing and risk-spreading behavior found between producers of finished automobiles and producers of automobile parts in Japan. We will show how the auto maker seeks to motivate the parts manufacturer's commitment to invest in necessary parts production for new car models through risk-sharing arrangements. In analyzing risk management, we will focus on the parts transfer-pricing scheme between automobile and parts manufacturers.

The automobile industry at this level consists of auto makers (final car assembly) and parts suppliers. In introducing a new model car, auto makers ask parts manufacturers to invest in the parts suitable for the new model. Thus, the parts supplier must invest in

* A revision of a paper first published in the *Journal of Business Administration*, 1987/88, Vol. 17, Nos. 1 & 2, pp. 117-136. Reprinted with kind permission of the University of British Columbia.
** This chapter was co-authored by Teruya Nagao, Information and Decision Sciences, University of Tsukuba.

appropriate facilities to make the parts and, as a result, accrue the fixed costs of these facilities.

Assuming that this particular investment project promises a high expected return, the parts supplier still risks covering the fixed costs of the investment. Whether or not the supplier can cover the fixed costs of parts for a new model car depends on the evolving market demand for the model. The auto maker also risks certain fixed costs for a new model production run. In other words, both auto maker and parts supplier risk covering certain segments of total fixed costs in new model car production.

If the supplier's management feels it is impractical to cover the total incremental fixed costs, the supplier may not make an adequate investment in the production facilities for this part. If the auto maker provides a subsidy in such a situation, the parts supplier's risk is defrayed and production becomes more likely. In this case, a certain degree of risk shifts from the supplier to the auto maker. The supplier, however, cannot expect as much profit later if the new car model is successful. On the other hand, if the parts supplier feels justified in covering the total fixed costs, there is no need for auto maker subsidies. In such a case, risk does not shift to the auto maker and the supplier's expected profit is higher.

In both cases, the auto maker's purpose is to motivate the parts manufacturer to make a commitment to invest in production. In this way, the parts necessary for a new model car can be obtained. In the Japanese auto industry, such risk-management control systems utilize transfer pricing for auto parts. We will describe how a certain system of subsidies and transfer prices can bring about risk sharing between the auto makers and the parts suppliers.

Transfer pricing is often based on a "full-cost-plus-markup" method. When based on the full-cost principle, the actual fixed overhead cost per unit of the transferred product will vary, depending on its sales volume. Therefore, the predetermined transfer price may not cover total fixed costs. Thus, under full cost-based transfer pricing, there is the persistent risk of uncovered fixed costs.

The risk-sharing behavior of a divisional firm was first analyzed by Kanodia (1979). Loeb and Magat (1978) and Harris, Kriebel, and Raviv (1982) have also characterized the systems of profit allocation and transfer pricing among divisions and central headquarters under asymmetric information situations. We will not examine the optimal full-cost transfer pricing system in the presence of either full or asymmetric information, but we will describe how supplementing such a system with direct subsidies allows risk sharing to occur.

First, we will introduce institutional aspects of general transfer-pricing practices for Japanese auto parts and then describe these practices in a set of hypothetical examples. Description of the institutional arrangements is based on Asanuma (1984) and Monden (1983, 1986).

Characteristics of Vertical Relationships in the Auto Industry. Development programs for both new cars and fully revamped models normally take about three years. During this development period, the specifications and blueprints of parts, part prices, and target costs of parts manufactured in-house as well as purchased parts are determined. The parts supplier and part price, which the authors call the "transfer price," are usually determined just before trial mass production, six to nine months before general mass production begins.

This part price will be used as a base price throughout the period of the part's mass production. As conditions change, however, price adjustments may be reached, usually at six-month intervals. Production periods for parts normally run four years for a full model change and two years for a minor model change. It should be noted that the engine and transmission are not necessarily changed for a full model change. Once orders are placed with a supplier to make a certain part, the supplier is hired for the full four- or two-year production cycle.

Compared to the frequency of price adjustments, quantity adjustments are made more often. First, to determine the initial base price, the estimated sales quantity of a part will be projected for the model life. Then, quantities will be computed monthly and requisitioned by applying the material requirement planning (MRP) system to the master production schedule of finished automobiles, based on quantities estimated by the dealerships. In addition, minor quantity adjustments may be made daily, based on daily orders from the dealers, four days or a week before car production begins.

This daily adjusted quantity is transmitted to the supplier by using the *kanban* system of sequence scheduling cards for the mixed-parts assembly line. The result is the just-in-time (JIT) production of cars in the required models and quantities at the exact time they are needed.

To summarize the nature of vertical relationships in the Japanese auto industry, the overall customer-vendor relationship is generally unlimited in duration. At the least, the parts supplier's position of selling a specific part to the auto maker will be maintained for the model life of the part. The price of the part, however, may be adjusted every six months through negotiation, and the general contract for a specific part may be discontinued after four years, in the case of a full model change, or after two years, in the case of a minor model change. In this sense, a "market" can be seen at each six-month interval, and again at each contract's expiration date.

Thus, the Japanese auto industry is an institutionalized system with both strong vertical relationships and competitive market characteristics. The authors call this system "market-adjusted organizational cooperation" or a "market-adjusted coalition."[1] In this sense, we use the term "transfer price" rather than market price.

In such a system, the autonomy of decisions by each supplier is weakened and quantity decisions are made by the auto maker. A fixed and continuous relationship as a parts supplier will be created, however, to minimize various transaction costs. Since the automobile manufacturer is free to discontinue contracts at their expiration date, the manufacturer can decrease management costs, which may take the form of a parts supplier's reluctance or inability to adopt requested environmental and technical innovations. On the other hand, a parts supplier maintains autonomy in the following areas:

- *Improvement activities and rationalized investment:* Improvements may be made in (1) working methods that reduce labor hours, (2) the utilization of materials and machines, and (3) facilities investments that reduce fixed labor costs.
- *Value engineering (VE) and value analysis (VA) resulting in design improvements.* Parts can be reformed and materials exchanged while still maintaining the same function or

quality level, thereby reducing the number of processes and the material costs. VE is conducted before, and VA after, mass production of the model begins.

As noted, negotiations on part prices will be conducted between the supplier and the auto maker every six months. In cases of improvements or savings, however, the total surplus created must be shared between the parts supplier and the auto maker. Otherwise, the supplier will lose incentive. Any surplus achieved through improvements may be (1) shared by the supplier, (2) retained in full by the supplier for six months or a year, or (3) absorbed in full by the auto maker for the time being, but evaluated during the regular price negotiations with preference shown to the parts supplier in question over competitive suppliers.[2]

Two Types of Parts Suppliers. The part price, or transfer price, of a part supplied from a vendor to an auto maker is determined and altered in one of two ways, depending on the type of parts supplier. Parts manufacturers can be divided into two general groups (Asanuma, 1984). The first has responsibility for machining and parts production manufacturing services, without involvement in design. In Japan, this is known as a *taiyo-zu*, or "borrowed blueprint maker." In such cases, the auto maker designs the part and farms out the production work.

The second type of parts supplier sometimes develops parts, submitting blueprints to the auto maker. If the designs are approved, the supplier can provide both design and manufacturing services to the auto maker. In Japan, such a supplier is called a *shonin-zu*, or "approved blueprint maker." Typically, borrowed blueprint makers supply the small pressed parts surrounding the auto body, while approved blueprint makers produce specialized parts, such as the battery, carburetor, electronic apparatus, ball-bearings, tires, and brakes.

Auto makers and parts suppliers can withhold information from one another. In practice, however, this asymmetric information-sharing, or risk-sharing, in Japan is rare. For the borrowed blueprint maker, there is a symmetry of information in which the auto maker's purchasing department is well aware of the parts supplier's facilities, capacity, workforce, costs, and required labor hours for each part. The auto maker allocates orders with full knowledge of each supplier's plant capacity. Because the supplier's internal information is well known, and also because the supplier lacks the ability to develop the part or parts in question, his profits tend to be smaller.

On the other hand, an asymmetry of information exists between the approved blueprint supplier and auto maker; that is, the details and breakdown of part costs are not fully disclosed to auto makers because the supplier is a developer of the part. Therefore, he can enjoy larger profits in negotiating prices. The transfer price proposed by such a supplier may be regarded as data implicitly disclosing the supplier's true state (Harris, Kriebel, and Raviv, 1982).

In practice, however, many parts suppliers lie between these two types of vendors. In such cases, parts are developed and designed jointly by both the auto maker and the supplier. Interior parts are often produced this way. While the plastic parts around the dashboard are generally designed by the auto maker, seats are often produced with design approval. In fact, both kinds of parts may be developed cooperatively once their general style is approved.

Two Types of Risk Arrangements Between an Auto Maker and a Parts Supplier. The transfer price of a certain part is calculated by the formula in Table 9-1. This formula is essentially based on the full-cost-plus-markup approach. From the formula, let's examine how the die cost average (e) is calculated.

Table 9-1. The Transfer Price of a Pressed Part

Transfer Price = (a + b + c + d) + e + (f + g + h)
a = Materials cost
b = Purchased parts
c = Outside processing costs
d = In-house processing costs (direct labor costs + overhead costs)
e = Die cost (depreciation cost of the dies)
f = Sales costs + administrative costs
g = Target profit
h = Savings through proposed improvements

The legal duration, based on depreciation for tax purposes, for die presses in Japan is two years. Estimated production levels for the two-year period must be projected to determine the die cost. Thus, the auto maker must inform the parts supplier of the estimated output level in a form of, for example, "20,000 units per month for the next two years."

Assume the estimated production quantity of a part is 480,000 units (20,000 units × 24 months). Therefore, the die cost per unit part will be:

$$e = \frac{x}{480,000} \text{ , where } x = \text{total cost of dies purchased}$$

The die cost of a part's transfer price is an interesting point in Japan. How die cost is handled depends on the parts supplier's function, that is, whether he is responsible for manufacturing only, or for both design and manufacturing. If the (e) amount calculated by the supplier is accepted and production of the part is stopped after two years because of a model change, a borrowed blueprint maker might be faced with one of two situations:

1. If car sales were below estimated levels, the cumulative output of the part at the end of two years may be less than projected, say, only 380,000 units. Where the (e) value was set to compensate for total die depreciation costs over 480,000 units, a portion of the die costs is unrecovered (in this case 20.8 percent or 100,000/480,000). In this situation, the auto maker generally will compensate the supplier for the unrecovered depreciation cost. This arrangement is, in essence, a contract in which the auto maker (principal) provides full insurance to the supplier (agent) against unforeseen fluctuations in demand. In other words, the auto maker covers the risk by giving a lump-sum subsidy to the supplier. This subsidy may be interpreted as an increase in transfer price value at the end of the period.

2. Suppose, however, that car sales were better than expected, increasing the cumulative output level to 480,000 units after only eighteen months (six months earlier than expected). In this situation, the transfer

price must be reduced by the amount of the unit die cost through renegotiation. As a result, the supplier generally cannot enjoy any extra profit for selling more parts than budgeted.

In these situations, we assume that the part is used only for a specific car of a particular auto maker.

In summary, the flexibility of the value of the transfer price depends on customer demand for the assembled car. The borrowed blueprint maker will have neither a loss nor extra profit in terms of die-cost compensation. It is the auto maker who either absorbs the loss or enjoys extra profit — because the auto maker carries the risk. This situation, therefore, implies that the parts supplier receives a subsidy equivalent to the total die costs. Similarly, aluminum die and mold subsidies are based on the number of pressings. Specialized machine subsidies are based on the estimated production quantity over the legal depreciation period of four years.

Another rule applies to the approved blueprint supplier: the risk of investing in dies for parts should be undertaken by the parts supplier, thereby making part price changes independent of the auto maker's demands.

This rule assumes that the part in question is one commonly used by various auto makers, making the risk from unforeseen demand fluctuations spread out over a number of manufacturers. If production of a certain part consists of something used exclusively by a particular auto maker and something used commonly by many auto makers, the former portion cost is guaranteed, while the latter portion cost has no such assurance.

A Simple Illustration of Risk Management Schemes. We shall now present a few models to illustrate the essentials of our discussion. Our illustrations will be presented in extremely simplified components — a linear utility measure and simple Bernoulli probability distribution. More sophisticated and formal arguments of our assertions can be presented with a variety of utility and probability terms, but not within the scope of this chapter.

Proposition 1. Suppose a parts supplier expects to realize profits that will fluctuate because of uncertain market demands for automobiles. Also assume that, although the supplier holds total risk, the auto maker chooses to share the supplier's risk by subsidizing a portion of the investment. In this way, fluctuations in the supplier's profits will be reduced, while expected profit remains unchanged. The supplier's risk is reduced, thus ensuring a more positive use of profits and perhaps inducing the supplier to accept a contract with the auto maker.

Illustrative Model for Proposition 1. Assumption 1: We assume that the utility (U) felt by the supplier for the monetary amount of profit (Y) can be depicted by the following simplified function:

$$U = Y \text{ for } Y \geqslant 0$$

$$U = kY \text{ for } Y < 0$$

In all the following cases, k is arbitrarily set at 4. The concavity of the previous utility functions implies that parts suppliers are susceptible to high losses.

Assumption 2: We may specify the situation of the supplier as yielding high profit and low profit with equal probability. At high demand, the sales quantity of the part should be 255 units; at low demand, 245 units.

We shall now present three cases: cases I(a) and I(b) for describing the situation of a borrowed blueprint maker, and case II for that of an approved blueprint maker. We will begin by demonstrating how the standard deviation of profits will be reduced when a subsidy is received.

Case I(a). Assumption 3: Suppose the supplier has the following data for making the parts in question.

- unit variable costs = $2.00
- fixed costs A = $690.00
- fixed costs B = $300.00
- unit margin = $0.04

(i) At average demand of high sales (225) units and low sales (245 units):

expected sales quantity = (225 + 245)/2 = 250 units

$$\text{transfer price} = (\$2 + \frac{\$690 + \$300}{250}) + \$0.04$$

$$= \$6$$

average profits = transfer price × volume − (total variables costs + fixed costs)

$$= \$6 \times 250 - (\$2 \times 250 + [\$690 + 300])$$

$$= \$10$$

Using the transfer price of $6.00, we will achieve the following two profit possibilities.

(ii) If high demand = 225 units:

high profits = transfer price × volume − total costs

$$= \$6 \times 255 - (\$2 \times 255 + [\$690 + \$300])$$

$$= \$30$$

(iii) If low demand = 245 units:

$$\text{low profits} = \$6 \times 245 - (\$2 \times 245 + [\$690 + \$300])$$

$$= -\$10$$

Since we assume a situation where only high and low profits occur with equal probability, the standard deviation of profit S^1 (y^1) will be:

$$S_1(y_1) = \sqrt{\frac{([-\$10 - \$10]^2 + [\$30 - \$10]^2)}{2}}$$

$$= \$20$$

We then get

$$E(U) = \frac{1}{2} \times 4 \times (\$10 - \$20) + \frac{1}{2} \times 1 \times (\$10 + \$20)$$

$$= -\$5$$

Here, the parts supplier's negative expected utility of profit implies that he would be reluctant to undertake production (see Figure 9-1). However, if the auto maker subsidizes the parts supplier,

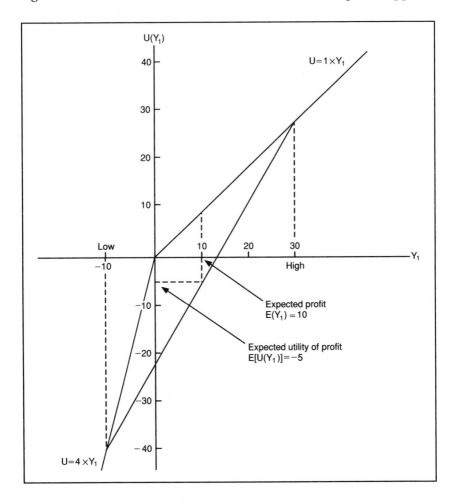

Figure 9-1. Case I (a)

as is done in Japan for borrowed blueprint makers, the figures in the example will be changed as follows.

Case I(b). Assumption 4: Suppose that fixed cost B is a die cost and will be compensated in full by a subsidy from the auto maker.[3]

(i) The transfer price and total revenue at average demand will essentially be:

Effective transfer price = unit variable costs ($2.00)

$$+ \text{ unit fixed costs A } \left(\frac{\$690}{250 \text{ units}} \right)$$

$$+ \text{ unit margin } (\$0.04)$$

$$= \$2 + \$2.76 + \$0.04$$

$$= \$4.80$$

Total average revenue = transfer price

$$\times \text{ average volume } + \text{ subsidy}$$

$$= \$4.80 \times 250 + 300$$

$$= \$1,500$$

Average profits = average revenue − average expenses

$$= \$1,500 - \$2 \times 250 + (\$690 + \$300)$$

$$= \$10$$

(ii) If high demand = 255 units:

high profits = ($4.80 × 255 + $300)

$$- \$2 \times 255 + (\$690 + \$300)$$

$$= \$24$$

(iii) If low demand = 245 units

low profits = ($4.80 × 245 + $300) − $2 × 245 + ($690 + $300)

= −$4

Again, since we are assuming that high and low profits will accrue with equal probability, the standard deviation of profit $S_2(y_2)$ will be:

$$S_2(y_2) = \sqrt{\frac{([-\$4 - \$10]^2 + [\$24 - \$10]^2)}{2}}$$

$$= \$14$$

Comparing case I(b) with case I(a), you will notice that the standard deviation was reduced to $14.00 from $20.00 while expected profits remained unchanged. Here we see the reduced risk of the supplier, who can receive a subsidy in compensation for certain fixed costs, while fluctuations of sales quantities remain unchanged.

The auto maker can subsidize the supplier's investment on the condition that the auto maker's preference is risk-neutral or less risk-averse, enabling that company to absorb a portion of the supplier's risk. Aversion to risk might be reduced for the Japanese auto maker because of his or her scale of operation and financial arrangements with the domestic banking community. We can calculate the expected utility for this modified situation with the following formula:

$$E(U) = \frac{1}{2} \times 4 \times (-\$4) + \frac{1}{2}$$

$$= \$4$$

Since the expected utility is of positive value, the supplier might decide to invest in this contract, as shown in Figure 9-2. The decision differs because a portion of the risk is shifted away from the supplier to the auto maker through subsidization. In other words, the auto maker guarantees recovery of die costs, while the parts supplier still bears the risk of the other items shown in Table 9-1. But the auto maker, as a result, can induce the supplier to participate in a coalition for manufacturing a new car model.

We now turn to case II, where we present a different type of supplier, one who has already contracted to supply a certain part to

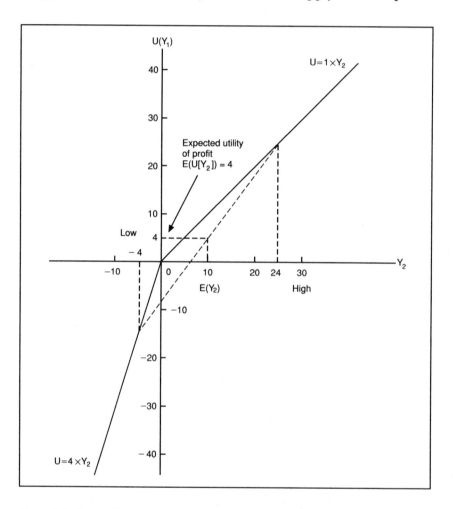

Figure 9-2. Case I (b)

auto maker I, and is now considering whether or not to sign a new contract to supply auto maker II with the same part.

Proposition 2. If a parts supplier already has contract I with a certain auto maker,[4] the supplier is likely to accept another independent contract II with a second auto maker, even though there is no subsidy for this additional contract. It does not seem worthwhile to accept contract II unless contract I is already in process. The degree of risk aversion or risk tolerance has decreased because of the ability to diversify risk over two manufacturers. As a result, the expected utility of contract II plus existing contract I tends to be positive. The variable coefficient of total profits from contracts I and II becomes smaller when both contracts are adopted, implying a reduction in risk.

Illustrative Model for Proposition II. Assumption 5: For simplicity, we assume the same utility function as assumption 1 and the same distribution of profits as Assumption 2 for both contracts I and II. We also assume that they are independent (that is, not correlated) so that we have a joint distribution, as in Table 9-2. Thus,

Profit from contract I: Y_1
Profit from contract II: Y_2
Total profit: $\quad\quad\quad Y = Y_1 + Y_2$
Utility function: $\quad U(Y) = U(Y_1 + Y_2)$

$$= 1 \times (Y_1 + Y_2) \text{ for } Y_1 + Y_2 \geq 0$$
$$\text{or } 4 \times (Y_1 + Y_2) \text{ for } Y_1 + Y_2 \leq 0$$

Table 9-2. Joint Probability Distribution, Case II (a)

	Y_1, or profit from contract I	Low	High
Y_2, or profit from contract II		(−10)	(30)
low (−10)		1/4	1/4
high (30)		1/4	1/4

Case II Data. Assumption 6: The cost data and unit margin for contracts I and II are the same as in Assumption 3. Therefore,

Expected profit from contract I: $E(Y_1) = \$10$
Standard deviation of profit from contract I: $S_1 = \$20$
Expected profit from contract II: $E(Y_2) = \$10$
Standard deviation of profit from contract II: $S_2 = \$20$

Thus, the distribution of joint profits $(Y_1 + Y_2)$ and total utility $U(Y_1 + Y_2)$ accruing from contracts I and II will be as depicted in Figure 9-3. For example, at a point $(high_1, low_2) = (30, -10)$ since $(high_1 + low_2) = 20$, the total utility (U) will be: $U = 1 \times Y = 1 \times (Y_1 + Y_2) = 1 \times (30 - 10) = \$20.00$.

As such, the calculation of expected utility for case II (the approved blueprint maker) will be:

$$E[U(Y)] = \overset{4}{\underset{\Sigma}{}} p_i k_i (Y^i_1 + Y^i_2)$$

$$\text{where } k_i = 1 \text{ for } Y_i + Y_2 \geq 0$$

$$k_i = 4 \text{ for } Y_1 + Y_2 < 0$$

$$p_i = \text{probability for joint profit}$$

Therefore,

$$E[U(Y)] = \tfrac{1}{4} \times 1 \times [high_1 + high_2]$$

$$+ \tfrac{1}{4} \times 1 \times [high_1 + high_2]$$

$$+ \tfrac{1}{4} \times 1 \times [low_1 + high_2]$$

$$+ \tfrac{1}{4} \times 4 \times [low_1 + high_2]$$

$$= \tfrac{1}{4} \times 1 \times [(\$10 + \$20) + (\$10 + \$20)]$$

$$+ \tfrac{1}{4} \times 1 \times [(\$10 + \$20) + (\$10 - \$20)]$$

$$+ \tfrac{1}{4} \times 1 \times [(\$10 - \$20) + (\$10 + \$20)]$$

$$+ \tfrac{1}{4} \times 4 \times [(\$10 - \$20) + (\$10 - \$20)]$$

$$= \$5$$

As a result, the approved blueprint maker will decide to accept contract II.

The reason we have a positive value of expected utility is that we achieved risk spreading. When the parts supplier accepts both contracts I and II as diversified investments, then expected profit from joint contracts is:

$$E(Y_1 + Y_2) = E(Y_1) + E(Y_2)$$
$$= \$10 + \$10$$
$$= \$20$$

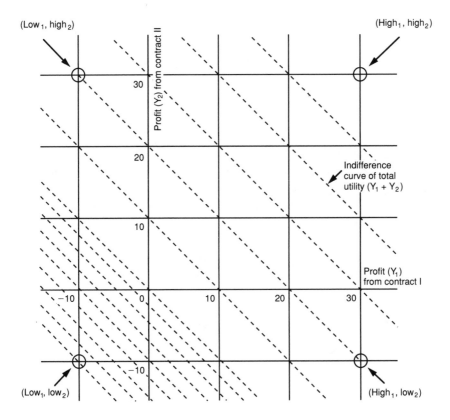

Figure 9-3. Distribution of Profits by Means of Contracts I and II

The standard deviation of profits from the joint contracts is:

$$S(Y_1 + Y_2) = \sqrt{S_1(Y_1)^2 + S_2(Y_2)^2 + 2S_1(Y_1) \times S_2(Y_2) \times r}$$
$$= \sqrt{(\$20)^2 + (\$20)^2 + 2 \times \$20 \times \$20 \times r}$$
$$= \$28.30 > S_2(Y_2)$$
$$= \$20$$

where r (the correlation coefficient) is assumed to be zero.Thus, the variation coefficient $S(Y)/E(Y)$ was reduced to 1

$$\frac{(28.3}{20)}$$

from the original 2

$$\frac{(20}{10)}$$

in just the single investment in contract I or II. This reduction in the variation coefficient was caused by risk spreading (instead of risk sharing) through the simultaneous adoption of two contracts. Another reduction in the variation coefficient implies decreased risk on the supplier's side.

Finally, we shall modify Assumption 5, which states that the distribution of Y_1 and Y_2 are independent, and test for the probability of Y_1 and Y_2 being somewhat correlated (see Table 9-3).

Table 9-3. Joint Probability Distribution, Case II (b)

Y_2 \ Y_1	Low	High
Low	$\frac{(1 + r)}{4}$	$\frac{(1 - r)}{4}$
High	$\frac{(1 - r)}{4}$	$\frac{(1 + r)}{4}$

If the correlation

coefficient $(r) = \frac{1}{3}$, then $E[U(Y)] = 0$

Conversely, if outcomes of Y_1, Y_2 have negative correlation, say,

$(r) = -\frac{1}{2}$, then $E[U(Y)] = \$12.50$

Therefore, it follows that the break-even point in the values of the correlation coefficient is $1/3$, if we assume all things are equal. In all likelihood, auto makers need not share manufacturing risk to motivate a parts supplier to participate in new car model production.

Conclusion. We have set out to clarify the different types of parts suppliers, the interrelationships between such suppliers and auto makers, and the overall risk-bearing behavior within the Japanese auto industry. The distinct differences in auto maker relationships between borrowed and approved blueprint parts suppliers, along with certain risk-sharing arrangements described here (such as the treatment of uncovered fixed costs), may be more prevalent in Japan than elsewhere. We have also paid particular attention to the formulation of transfer pricing based on full-cost consideration and to the transfer price flexibility used by auto makers to stimulate supplier investment.

In summary, the risk of the borrowed blueprint maker will be reduced by risk-sharing with the auto maker, which motivates the supplier to accept the contract. On the other hand, the approved blueprint maker can enter into multiple contracts and reduce risk on any contracts after the first. This behavior is also explained by the concept of risk spreading, a risk that need not be shared by auto makers.

10

Factory Automation and Cost Reduction at Daihatsu*

Although factory automation (FA) has a number of objectives, economic efficiency is the most important. This is expressed as increased productivity and reduced costs. Additional objectives are to achieve a stable product quality, production that is flexible vis-a-vis demand fluctuations, and a high regard for human work. In this respect, factory automation has made great inroads in strategic decision-making at top management levels.

This chapter examines factory automation's emphasis on the economic efficiency of accounting in the Japanese auto industry. The extent of FA development should become clear from the case study of Daihatsu Motor Company, based on a 1987 interview with Shigemi Takagi, assistant manager of the second production technology department.

Economic Efficiency Accounting and Decisions Regarding Factory Automation. *Has Daihatsu decided upon the length of time necessary to introduce factory automation systems in the future?*

---

* First published in *Kigyo kaikei* (Corporate accounting), 1989, Vol. 41, No. 2.

An economic life cycle usually covers two models. Since an automobile's life cycle is four or five years, for two models we think in terms of eight to ten years. In terms of the rationalization of investments, we regard the economic life cycle of such investments as one to two years. We are really talking about the case flow period required to determine the economic effect of investments. As far as a profit plan is concerned, we prepare mid-term profit plans covering a three-year period.

What standards have been adopted regarding the economic accounting of equipment investment?

For economic accounting, we use payback of capital methods. Decisions are made by comparing the amount of yearly recovery to the amount of investments and multiplying it by the capital payback coefficient. This method is usually applied only to equipment for small-lot production. It will be impossible to achieve efficient mass production until advances are made in large-lot automation. That is why, from a physical standpoint, automation is an indispensable requirement of economic accounting.

In addition, economic accounting sometimes encourages factory automation decisions based on different standards. These decision standards require improving equipment and operating conditions to achieve consistent product quality. For instance, when plant temperatures where operations are in progress become unbearable, or when people are overworked, manual labor must be replaced by machines — if the management has respect for the worker.

Specialized machines are another instance in which the application of economic accounting is demanded. For example, when a car model is modified, making it necessary to introduce a new specialized line of equipment, economic accounting is indispensable. On such occasions, sales estimates are vital. Since the life cycle of equipment decreases when minor model changes occur every two years, accounting must be strict. It becomes necessary to begin accounting procedures for the new model before actual production begins. This is how economic accounting is applied on a two-model life cycle.

General-purpose machines, on the other hand, can be used for twenty or thirty years with proper maintenance. A die press can be used for years to make dies for any model. This holds true for painting processes and conveyors on the assembly line. Nevertheless, while these machines might be used for decades, whether or not their performances continue to prove satisfactory is another issue.

Does the period of economic life cycle described in your answer to Question 1 include the expected payback period?

Yes. We consider the economic life cycle of general-purpose equipment to be eight to ten years, the expected payback period included. When investing in equipment for purposes of rationalization, the expected economic life cycle of such equipment is one to two years with an expected payback period of one to two years.

In your opinion, what is the most important merit of factory automation?

Factory automation reduces labor costs and improves the quality of our products.

From the standpoint of flexible response to demand fluctuations, which is more important — factory automation or workers?

As far as the number of workers is concerned, we can accommodate demand fluctuations by using measures designed to increase or decrease the number of workers — transferring people to other facilities, for instance. This is quite easy.

In automated operations, the rate of machine utilization is important. As factory automation is introduced, production capability must not decline; the cost per product unit would rise should the rate of machine utilization be low. In addition, when the needed production volume is higher than the existing manufacturing capability, it is necessary to change the system. For these reasons, flexibility is necessary.

At the same time, the flexibility needed to meet market demands for a wide variety of products means using flexible manufacturing system (FMS) machines designed for general use that can be adapted to diversified production. When demand fluctuations affect the production capacity of available equipment, some machines can be idle and ready when needed.

The human factor is more important in terms of the type of flexibility that is linked to fluctuating production quantities. This human factor, however, has its problems. Putting personnel to work every day requires monthly transfers, which make it difficult to create a good labor program. Also, labor costs are rising. Furthermore, once employed, workers are capable of performing for thirty or forty years. The amortization of machines, however, is completed in about ten years. Therefore, by observing demand fluctuations over time, we could say that the manufacturing capability of equipment — one that corresponds to market demand — can be accommodated every ten years.

After considering these issues, we feel it is necessary to promote further automation.

What factors are important when selecting factory automation devices?

The most important factor is cost, followed by quality and service.

Factory Automation: From Design to Introduction. *Did your own staff promote automation in your plants or did you turn to outside manufacturing specialists?*

Since our system design is industry-specific, only our workers would be able to understand it. For this reason, we entrusted our own personnel with this task. To convert this design to a computerized system, however, we relied on outside consultants.

Much of the standard equipment can be purchased easily from an outside manufacturer of such equipment and then introduced into the plants. Some machines, however, are produced in our plants for our own use. For instance, 60 to 70 percent of our welding robots are manufactured on the premises. On the other hand, the percentage of equipment ordered from outside suppliers is increasing gradually because of the rapid changes in FA technology. Auto makers must have the latest equipment in order to meet the changes that now occur in a matter of months — if not days.

What is the biggest obstacle to overcome when introducing factory automation?

The biggest problem is equipment maintenance — training maintenance personnel to keep the equipment running efficiently. Although the task of the equipment designers is very important, the role of the maintenance department is growing. In fact, the ranks of maintenance workers is increasing faster than that of equipment operators. Because we purchase a lot of equipment from other manufacturers, we were forced to rely on their maintenance people to fix machines that broke down. Now our goal is to produce as much equipment as possible in-house and rely on our own maintenance department.

In introducing office automation, obstacles revolve around existing conditions in the business environment at the time of introducing the factory automation equipment. Although FA systems clearly have their merits, when product demand is low and the labor ratio is high, factory automation becomes a difficult proposition.

Who is responsible for factory automation?

Traditionally, the head of the production technology department is responsible for factory automation. In Japan, however, it was proposed to make FA a bottom-up activity. In recent decision-making meetings dealing with new models, this was approved by the technology committees that are part of the top management structure. Likewise, the bottom-up approach was approved in production meetings held with top management regarding investment in the rationalization of equipment, plants, and buildings.

How long does it take for a decision about factory automation to be made and actual FA equipment to be introduced into the plant?

The time between decision and action can be two years — or three years, if we include the latest technology.

Please describe the various stages of factory automation and how long each stage lasts.

The first stage, from system design until the specifications are determined, takes about one year. The second stage, which is the developmental stage, lasts six to ten months. The third stage, trial operations, take five or six months. This makes a total time period of approximately two years.

Present Automation Conditions. *Please address the following five areas in terms of the extent to which automation has occurred in your company: (1) processing operations, (2) assembly operations, (3) transport of material, (4) setup operations, and (5) production planning?*

Automating Processing Operations. Pressing operations on the stamping line are fully automated. Stacking the pressed workpieces on palettes, however, is still done manually.

In welding operations, 80 percent of the spot welding is automated and 20 percent is done manually. Setting up the workpiece for the welding process and subsequently removing it, however, is done manually. These operations include one-touch programming and similar features. Once the workpiece is set up, operations are designed to be done automatically by machines. Human workers do not even push a button.

Welding operations on the main body line are also fully automated and completely unmanned.

Automating Assembly Operations. Automating the assembly operations generally lags behind, and only 5 percent of such operations have been automated. In assembly operations, (1) an object is picked up, (2) it is then fastened and processed, and (3) it is passed on. The assembly process consists of these three operations. Since a heavy automobile consists of 2,000 parts and three operations are required to assemble these parts, there are 6,000 required assembly operations. To date, at our company's most advanced plant, we have automated 5 percent of these 6,000 operations. Our goal is to automate 7 to 10 percent of our assembly operations.

To speed up the automation of our assembly operations, the construction and assembly of the automobile must be simplified. We are promoting the standardization of models and parts, including the joint use of parts for different models, and converting to panel assembly. Panel assembly is simplified assembly. For example, if there are 100 screws in a group of parts to be assembled, we first assemble a body shell off the moving assembly line. Later, only four or five screws are required for use on the moving assembly line.

At the moment, fully automating assembly operations in automobile manufacturing is difficult. Most companies in the industry have been unable to automate more than 5 percent of their assembly lines. Constructing an automobile flows from the bottom up, and these types of operations can be automated easily. The difficulty lies in automating the assembly process because assembly is about setting positions. Particularly difficult assembly operations are those that involve automating the fastening of bolts on parts moving on conveyor lines. In this area of operations, assembling parts in a previous step of the process (the "cassette method") becomes increasingly important.

Automating the Transport of Material. We have made a lot of progress in automating the steps between individual processes. We have successfully automated the transport of parts from the body line to the painting line and from the painting line to the assembly line. All the material is handled by conveyers.

Automating the handling of material that is transported from the pressing plant to the body plant, (that is, automating the handling of material between plants) still lags behind.

Automating Setup Operations. By distinguishing between "internal" and "external" setup procedures, it is possible to automate the die changeover process by developing a process that can be handled by pushing a button. In other words, internal setup can be handled automatically by the die press.

Because a crane is used with the die press for external setup, the time required for external setup is relatively long. The changeover time can be shortened by reducing the lot size. The time required for external setup can be shortened by using two cranes, but the number of operators is doubled. This would still shorten the time required from 30 minutes to 15 minutes. A more important priority, however, is to reduce the number of workers.

Automating Production Planning. A plant's central control room is provided with computerized assembly line control (ALC) devices that indicate the status of production on a software program. The ALC provides information on the progress of processes occurring on the body, painting, and assembly lines. For instance, the line computer that controls operations on the body assembly line will automatically replace welding equipment in response to the flow of various types of body units. In addition, numbers that indicate the body line's 100 processes are displayed by the ALC on digital display panels, enabling the operator to understand what is going on at any given moment.

Glossary

As a guide to understanding some of the concepts discussed in this book, the editor defines some basic terminology used in discussing the new manufacturing environment. She gratefully acknowledges the works of Taiichi Ohno (*Toyota Production System: Beyond Large-scale Production*, 1988) and Brian Maskell (*Performance Measurement for World Class Manufacturing: A Model for American Companies*, 1991) in compiling this information.

Andon. *Andon*, the line-stop indicator board hung above the production line, is a visual control. The trouble indicator light works as follows:

When operations are normal, the *green light* is on. When workers want to adjust something on the line and call for help, they turn on a *yellow light*. If a line stop is needed to rectify a problem, the *red light* is turned on. To thoroughly eliminate abnormalities, workers should not be afraid to stop the line.

Autonomation. The Toyota production system utilizes *autonomation*, or automation with a human touch, rather than automation. Autonomation means transferring human intelligence to a machine. The concept originated with the auto-activated loom of Toyota founder and inventor, Sakichi Toyoda. His invention was equipped with a device that automatically stopped the machine if vertical or lateral threads broke or ran out. In other words, a device capable of making a judgment was built into the machine.

At Toyota, this concept is applied not only to the machinery but also to the production line and the workers. In other words, if an abnormal situation arises, a worker is required to stop the line. Autonomation prevents the production of defective products, eliminates overproduction, and automatically stops abnormalities on the production line allowing the situation to be investigated.

Cycle Time *versus* Takt Time. In practical terms, *cycle time* is the length of time between when material for a product enters a plant and the point at which the finished product is shipped. Therefore, cycle time refers to the actual production capability of a plant. In contrast, *takt time* is the time frame that the market demands for a product. By distinguishing between cycle time and takt time, we gain a perception of the waste of overproduction and achieve the most effective use of labor.

Flexible Manufacturing System. A *flexible manufacturing system* (FMS) is an integrated system of tools and equipment that is designed to produce a variety of parts in small or medium quantities. In order to be flexible to significant changes in production volume, a company must have more capacity than demand. In contrast to a traditional manufacturer who always strives to reach higher levels of plant utilization, the new manufacturing environment requires a company's plants to have spare capacity so that changes in market demands can be more easily accommodated.

Inventory Reduction. Inventory reduction is a cornerstone of the new manufacturing environment and many JIT techniques are aimed at bringing inventories down, including raw material, component, work-in-process, and finished goods inventories. There are several ways to measure inventory levels, such as stock turns or the number of days of stock. Although stock turns is expressed as a nonfinancial measure, it is calculated from the financial measures of inventory valuation and cost of goods sold.

Just-In-Time. With the possibility of acquiring products at the time and in the quantity needed, waste, unevenness, and unreasonableness can be eliminated and efficiency improved. Kiichiro-

Toyoda, the father of Japanese car manufacturing, originally conceived this idea, which his successors then developed into a production system. The thing to remember is that it is not only "in time" but "just in time." *Just-in-time* and *autonomation* constitute the two main pillars of the Toyota production system.

Kanban. A *kanban* (or tag) is a tool for managing and assuring just-in-time production, the first pillar of the Toyota production system. Basically, a kanban is a simple and direct form of communication always located at the point where it is needed. In most cases, a kanban is a small piece of paper inserted in a rectangular vinyl envelope. On this piece of paper is written how many of what part to pick up or which parts to assemble.

In the just-in-time method, a later process goes to an earlier process to withdraw needed goods, when and in the quantity needed. The earlier process then produces the quantity withdrawn. In this case, when the later process goes to the earlier process to pick up, they are connected by the withdrawal or transport information, called *withdrawal kanban* or *transport kanban*, respectively. This is an important role of kanban.

Another role is the *in-process*, or *production-ordering kanban*, which tells the operator to produce the quantity withdrawn from the earlier process. These two kanban work as one, circulating between the processes within Toyota, between the company and its outside suppliers, and also between the processes in each supplier.

In addition, there are *signal kanban* used in the stamping process, for instance, where production of a specific quantity, perhaps more than required by JIT, cannot be avoided.

Management Accounting. Traditional management accounting was developed during the industrial revolution and the early part of the twentieth century. The root cause of problems that many companies have with traditional management accounting is that management accounting techniques have not kept pace with the changes occurring in manufacturing.

Today's performance measurement system must support the company's manufacturing strategy in nonfinancial terms. The strategy will often refer to such financial goals as lowering costs, achieving margins, realizing returns on assets, or contributing to stock value. The majority of strategic factors, however, will be nonfinancial — such as quality, reliability, flexibility, innovation, lead time, customer satisfaction, and social issues.

Multiprocess Operation System. In the machining process, suppose, for example, that five lathes, five milling machines, and five drilling machines are lined up in two parallel rows. If an operator operates five lathes, we call this a multi-unit operation system. The same is true for handling five milling or five drilling machines.

If, however, an operator operates one lathe, one milling machine, and one drilling machine (that is, several processes), we call this a *multiprocess operation system*. In the Toyota production system, setting up the production flow is of primary importance. Therefore, we try to achieve multiprocess operations that directly reduce the number of workers. For the worker on the production line, this means shifting from being *single-skilled* to becoming *multiskilled*.

Production Leveling. On a production line, fluctuations in product flow increase waste. This is because the equipment, workers, inventory, and other elements required for production must always be prepared for peak production. If a later process varies its withdrawal of parts in terms of timing and quantity, the range of these fluctuations will increase as they move up the line toward earlier processes.

To prevent fluctuations in production even in outside suppliers, we must try to keep the fluctuation in final assembly to zero. Toyota's final assembly line never assembles the same automobile model in a batch. Production is *leveled* by making first one model, then another model, then yet another.

Small Lot Sizes and Quick Setups. In production leveling, batches are made as small as possible in contrast to traditional mass production, where bigger is considered better. Toyota tries to avoid assembling the same type of car in batches. Of course, when the final assembly process does produce this way, the earlier process — such as the press operation — naturally has to go along with it. This means die changes must occur frequently. Up to now, conventional wisdom has dictated having each die press punch out as many parts as possible. In the Toyota production system, however, this does not apply. Die changes are made quickly and improved even more with practice. In the 1940s, they took two to three hours. In the 1950s, they dropped from one hour to fifteen minutes. Recently, setups have been shortened to three minutes.

Toyota Production System. The first aspect of the Toyota production system is the *Toyota-style method of production*, which means putting a *flow* into the manufacturing process. In the past, lathes were located in the lathe area, and milling machines in the milling area. Now, we place a lathe, a milling machine, and a drilling machine in the actual sequence of the manufacturing process.

This way, instead of having one worker per machine, one worker oversees many machines or, more accurately, *one worker operates many processes.* This improves productivity.

Next is the *kanban* system, an operational tool that carries out the *just-in-time* production method. Kanban assures that the right parts are available at the time and in the quantity needed by functioning as the withdrawal or transport information, an order for conveyance or delivery of the goods and also as a *work order* within the production processes.

Value Engineering. Traditional accounting accountants spend a lot of time determining production costs. One reason is that the product cost is used to determine the sales price. In reality, product price in most industrial sectors is market-driven; in other words, product costs are what the market will bear.

In light of this, techniques have been developed that are designed to enable manufacturers to establish target prices and target costs in line with market needs. Some major Japanese companies pioneered a formal approach to the establishment of price and cost targets in the form of *value engineering* (VE). VE is an integral part of the design process within all divisions of the Toyota group of companies and is used in the earliest stages of new product development. The goal of value engineering is to use the expertise and ingenuity of people in the company to develop innovative ideas to bring a new product's cost into line with the allowed cost.

Visual Control (Management by Sight). Autonomation means stopping the production line or the machine whenever an abnormal situation arises. This clarifies what is normal and what is abnormal. In terms of quality, any defective products are forced to surface because the actual progress of work in comparison to daily production plans is always clearly visible. This idea applies to machines and the lines as well as to the arrangement of goods and tools, inventory, circulation of kanban, standard work procedures, and so on. In production lines using the Toyota production system, *visual control*, or management by sight, is enforced.

Work Flow. *Work flow* means that value is added to the product in each process while the product flows along. If goods are carried by conveyor, this is not work flow, but work forced to flow. The basic achievement of the Toyota production system is setting up the manufacturing flow. This naturally means establishing a work flow.

World Class Manufacturing. As companies introduce world class manufacturing techniques, they need new methods of performance measurement to control production plants. These new methods are needed because (1) traditional management accounting is not relevant to world class manufacturing, (2) customers are requiring higher standards of quality, performance, and flexibility, and (3) new management methods employed by world class manufacturers require different kinds of performance measures.

While different companies introduce world class manufacturing differently, the attributes always included are a new approach to quality, JIT manufacturing techniques, changes in managing the workforce, and a more flexible approach to meeting customer needs.

References and Notes

Chapter 2
(References)

Ban, Shoji and Kimura, Osamu. "Toyota Automobiles Production Department — Basic Principles with Built-in Flexibility," *JMA Production Management* (October 1986): 13-23.

Noto, Akira and Monden, Yasuhiro. *Daihatsu Industries — Cost Accounting in the Automobile Industry,* Kiyoshi Okamoto, Akira Miyamoto, and Michiharu Sakurai, coauthors.

Ohno, Taiichi (editor) and Monden, Yasuhiro (author). *New Developments in Toyota's Production Method* (Tokyo: Nihon Noritsu Kyokai, 1983).

Ryozumi, Takehiko. "The Selica System — until a New Model Is Developed," *Motor Fun* (January 1990): 31-48.

Tanaka, Takao. "Toyota's Kaizen Budget — Fundamentals of the Japanese Way of Budgetary Accounting," *Kigyō kaikei* (Corporate Accounting) (January 1990): Vol. 42, No. 3, 59-66.

Chapter 3
(Notes)

1. Refer to the following articles for recent investigations of cost control in the planning and design processes of new products:

Koura, K. "Product quality and economic efficiency," *Operations Research*, August 1981, 437-442.

Makito, T. "Current trends in Japan's cost control practice," *Enterprise Accounting*, March 1979, 126-132.

Nakamori, K. "Cost control of the design department (1) (2)," *Industrial Engineering*, November 1981, 65-70, and December, 58-64.

Tanaka, M. "Development of cost control — Cost control in technological decision-making processes," *Costing*, Vol. 255, December 1981, 3-32.

2. Aoki, S. "Functional management as top management: Examples of management concepts at Toyota," *Quality Control*, Vol. 32, No. 2, (92-98), No. 3, (66-71), No. 4, (65-69).

3. Makito, T. *op. cit.,* 132.

4. Refer to the following for the framework of the Toyota production system:

Monden, Y., "What makes the Toyota production system really tick?" *Industrial Engineering*, January 1981.

Monden, Y., *Toyota Production System*, American Institute of Industrial Engineers, 1983.

Chapter 5
(Notes)

1. Hunt, R., Garrett, L., and Merz, C.M. "Direct Labor Cost Not Always Relevant at HP," *Management Accounting*, (1985): 58-62.

2. Boer, Germain B. *Management Accounting: News and Views*, 5, No. 1 (1987): 1.

3. Monden, Yasuhiro, and Noboru, Yoshiteru. "Integrated Cost Control Systems in the Japanese Automotive Industry," *Kigyō kaikei* (Business Accounting) 35, No. 2 (1983). (A revised version of this article appears in *High Tech Accounting*, by Okamoto, Miyamoto, and Sakurai, eds. [Doyukan, 1988].)

Chapter 6
(Notes)

1. The description of MRP and its cost accounting system presented in this chapter was possible thanks to the valuable contributions of Kunio Fujimoto and Masakatsu Mori:

Fujimoto, K. "Serving the Big Manufacturers: How to Cope with Short Lead Time and Changing Delivery Schedules," APICS, 1980.

Fujimoto, K. "The Practice of MRP Progress," Nihon Noritsu Kyokai (Japan Efficiency Association), 1980.

Fujimoto, K. "American Methods of the Kanban System: "Revolution in the Factory Caused by MRP," Diamond Company, 1983.

Mori, M. "New Cost Control with Computers," *Kojo kanri* (Plant Management), Vol. 28, Nos. 2, 3, 4, 7, 8, 9, and 11, 1982.

2. In this regard, MRP implementation is of paramount importance, as stressed by R.W. Hall and T.W. Wollman in *Harvard Business Review* article "Planning Your Material Requirement" (September-October 1978).

3. Figure 6-1 was based on unpublished material ("MST and Production Control") from Hitachi's Sawa plant.

4. Excerpted from J. Masuyama's "FMS at Toyota, Its Interpretation and Practice" (ICPW proceedings, 1982).

5. According to Takeshita and Mori. As far as integration of MRP and the kanban method is concerned, other available reference materials include:

Hall, R.W. "Driving the Productivity Machine: Production Planning and Control in Japan" (APICS, 1981).

Mori, M., and Harmon, R.L. "Combining the Best of the West with the Best of the East: MRP and Kanban Working in Harmony" (APICS, 1980).

Yamada, Z. "The Gist of the Kanban-MRP System Design," *Kojo kanri* (Plant Management) (Vol. 29, No. 1, 1982).

Yamada, Z. "Kanban-MRP Systems: Designed to Link Control to Technology," *Kojo kanri* (Plant Management), (Vol. 30, No. 1, January 1984).

(References)

Monden, Y. *Toyota Production System*, (Norcross, GA: Industrial Engineering and Management Press, 1983).

Monden, Y. *Toyota System*, (Kodansha, 1985).

Monden, Y., ed. *Latest Developments in the Toyota Production*

System, (Tokyo: Japan Efficiency Association, 1983).

Takeshita, J., Mori, M. "New Production Control System PYMAC at Yamaha Motors," *Kojo kanri* (Plant Management), (Vol. 29, No. 1, January 1983).

Yoshitani, R., Nakane, K. "Toyota Production System from the Viewpoint of an MRP System Researcher," *Kojo kanri* (Plant Management), (Vo. 24, No. 13).

Yoshitani, R., Nakane, K. "MRP and the Kanban Method (1)," *News of the System Science Research Institute of the Waseda University,* (No. 32, 1978).

Yoshitani, R., Nakane, K. "MRP and the Kanban Method (2)," *News of the System Science Research Institute of the Waseda University,* (No. 10, 1979).

Yoshizawa, T. "What Is Expected from Cost Control and Cost Accounting Managers: Making 1980 the Year of MRP," *Genkan keisan* (Cost Accounting) (1980).

Chapter 7
(References)

Tani, Takeyuki. "Strategy, Organizational Structures, and Managerial Accounting Systems," *Kokumin keizai zashi* (National Economic Magazine), Vol. 159, Issue 5, 1989, 31-43.

Kato, Noboru. "The Production Mix in Four-Wheel-Drive Tractors" (TM-II), *Kojo kanri* (Plant Management), Vol. 30, Issue 11, (November 1984), 42-50.

Chapter 9
(Notes)

1. Imai et al. (1982) call this system an "intermediate organization." It may be considered a hybrid of a "syndicate" (defined by R. Wilson) and a "team" (defined by J. Marschak and R. Radner), where the whole system is regarded as a syndicate, with each company in it considered a team.

2. North American auto companies have maintained a high in-house manufacturing ratio of steel products and unit, or main assembly, parts. Although this approach may contribute to reduced market transaction costs, it could simultaneously increase management costs.

Recently, their in-house manufacturing ratio has begun to decrease.

3. The value of the transfer price will be decreased by the amount of unit die costs when the expected sales are realized earlier than planned. Also, the uncovered depreciation cost of dies will be compensated by the auto maker when the sales are below those expected. Therefore, such a convention implies that the part supplier receives a subsidy equivalent to the die cost.

4. Although the expected utility of contract I itself is negative, the reader can assume that its negative value of utility is discovered only after the contract is adopted.

(References)

Asanuma, B. (1984). *Jidosha sangyo niokeru buhin torihiki no kozo: chosei to kakushinteki tekio no mechanism* ("The Organization of Parts Purchases in the Japanese Automotive Industry"), *Kikan Gendai Keizai*, No. 58, pp. 38-48.

Harris, M. Kriebel., C. H., and Raviv, A. (1982). "Asymmetric Information, Incentives, and Intrafirm Resource Allocation," *Management Science*, Vol. 28, No. 6, 604-620.

Imai, K., Itami H., and Koike, K. (1982). *Naibu-soshiki no neizaigaku* ("Economics of Internal Organization"), (Tokyo: Toyokeizai-Shinposha Publishers)

Kanodia, C. (1979) "Risk Sharing and Transfer Price System Under Uncertainty," *Journal of Accounting Research*, Vol. 16, No. 1, 103-121.

Loeb, M. and Magat, W.A. (1978). "Soviet Success Indicators and the Evaluation of Divisional Management," *Journal of Accounting Research*, Vol. 16, No. 1, 103-121.

Monden, Y. (1983). *Toyota Production System* (Norcross, GA: Industrial Engineering and Management Press).

Monden, Y. (1986). "Total Cost Management System in Japanese Automobile Corporations," *Applying Just-In-Time: The American/ Japanese Experience* (Norcross, GA: Industrial Engineering and Management Press), 171-184.

About the Author

Yasuhiro Monden is professor of managerial accounting and production management at the University of Tsukuba (Institute of Socio-economic Planning), Tsukuba-shi, Japan. He received his Ph.D. from the University of Tsukuba, where he also served as dean of the Graduate Program of Management Sciences and Public Policy Studies.

Dr. Monden has gained valuable practical knowledge and experience from his research and related activities in the Japanese automobile industry. He was instrumental in introducing the Just-In Time (JIT) production system to the United States. His English-language book, *Toyota Production System,* is recognized as a JIT classic; it was awarded the 1984 Nikkei Prize by the *Nikkei Economic Journal.*

Dr. Monden's international activities have included a visiting professorship at the State University of New York at Buffalo in 1980-81. He is currently a visiting professor at California State University, Los Angeles. He is also an advisor for the Production and Operations Management Society (POMS); has acted as an international director of the Management Accounting Section of the American Accounting Association, and currently serves on the editorial board of the AAA's *Journal of Management Accounting Research.*

Other Engish-language books written by Dr. Monden include: *Japanese Management Accounting* (Productivity Press, 1989); *Applying Just-In-Time: The American/Japanese Experience* (IIE, 1986); and *Innovations in Management: The Japanese Corporation* (IIE, 1985).

Index

173

OTHER BOOKS ON QUALITY

Productivity Press publishes and distributes materials on continuous improvement in productivity, quality, customer service, and the creative involvement of all employees. Many of our products are direct source materials from Japan that have been translated into English for the first time and are available exclusively from Productivity. Supplemental products and services include newsletters, conferences, seminars, in-house training and consulting, audio-visual training programs, and industrial study missions. Call 1-800-274-9911 for our free book catalog.

Japanese Management Accounting
A World Class Approach to Profit Management
edited by Yasuhiro Monden

Just as the Japanese redefined manufacturing excellence, so they have transformed management accounting in world class companies. Here is a comprehensive overview of the Japanese approach to management accounting, especially helpful for companies that have adopted Just-In-Time manufacturing. More than thirty chapters discuss how to account for, and reduce, costs in every area of the company, from the plant and warehouse to design and planning. This unprecedented inside view reveals different strategic approaches to profit planning in Japan and shows how they can be adapted to American needs.
ISBN 0-915299-50-x / 568 pages / $ 59.95 / Order code JMACT-BK

TQC for Accounting
A New Role in Company-wide Improvement
by Takashi Kanatsu

TQC for accounting means more than streamlining office procedures or upgrading finacial analysis. It requires, instead, a linking of the basics of marketing with the fundamentals of accounting through the medium of TQC. This book is a guide for top and middle managers who wish to turn their companies around by redesigning the roles played by the accounting, sales, and marketing departments. The book's format offers detailed examinations of accounting TQC in relation to a company's business plan, accounting department, and specific statistical methods. Its use will help to create the "awareness revolution" that is imperative in turning around a factory or any type of company.
ISBN 0-915299-73-9 / 176 pages / $ 45.00 / Order code TQCA-BK

Productivity Press, Inc., Dept. BK, P.O. Box 3007, Cambridge, MA 02140 1-800-274-9911

Quality Function Deployment
Integrating Customer Requirements into Product Design
Yoji Akao (ed.)

More and more, companies are using quality function deployment, or QFD, to identify their customers' requirements, translate them into quantified quality characteristics and then build them into their products and services. This casebook introduces the concept of quality deployment as it has been applied in a variety of industries in Japan. The materials include numerous case studies illustrating QFD applications. Written by the creator of QFD, this book provides direct source material on Quality Function Deployment, one of the essential tools for world class manufacturing. It is a design approach based on the idea that quality is determined by the customer. Through methodology and case studies the book offers insight into how Japanese companies identify customer requirements and describes how to translate customer requirements into qualified quality characteristics, and how to build them into products and services.
ISBN 0-915299-41-0 / 400 pages / $ 75.00 / Order code QFD-BKHandbook of Quality Tools

Handbook of Quality Tools
The Japanese Approach
Tetsuichi Asaka and Kazuo Ozeki (eds.)

The Japanese have stunned the world by their ability to produce top quality products at competitive prices. This comprehensive teaching manual, which includes the 7 traditional and 5 newer QC tools, explains each tool, why it's useful, and how to construct and use it. Information is presented in easy-to-grasp language, with step-by-step instructions, illustrations, and examples of each tool. A perfect training aid, as well as a hands-on reference book, for supervisors, foremen, and/or team leaders. Here's the best resource on the myriad Japanese quality tools changing the face of world manufacturing today. Accessible to everyone in your organization, dealing with both management and shop floor how-to's, you'll find it an indispensable tool in your quest for quality.
ISBN 0-915299-45-3 / 336 pages / $59.95 / Order code HQT-BK

Productivity Press, Inc., Dept. BK, P.O. Box 3007, Cambridge, MA 02140 1-800-274-9911

Managerial Engineering
Techniques for Improving Quality and Productivity in the Workplace (rev.)
Ryuji Fukuda

A proven path to managerial success, based on reliable methods developed by one of Japan's leading productivity experts and winner of the coveted Deming Prize for quality. Dr. W. Edwards Deming, world-famous consultant on quality, says that the book "provides an excellent and clear description of the devotion and methods of Japanese management to continual improvement of quality." (CEDAC® training programs also available.)
ISBN 0-915299-09-7 / 208 pages / $39.95 / Order code ME-BK

TQC Solutions
A 14-Step Process
JUSE Problem Solving Research Group (ed.)

Foreword by Dr. H. James Harrington

Here's a clear-cut, thoroughly explained process for putting the tools of quality control to work in your company. With a strong emphasis on the use of quality control in problem solving, this book was originally written as a handbook for the Union of Japanese Scientists and Engineers' (JUSE) renowned Quality Control seminar. Filled with practical, highly useful information, it shows you not only *how* to use the 7 QC tools, the 7 "new" QC tools, and basic statistical tools, but also suggests *when* to use them. The use of charts and matrices in problem solving is carefully examined and illustrated with examples of various problems and their solutions.
ISBN 0-915299-79-8 / 448 pages, 2 volumes / $120.00 / Order TQCS-BK

TQC Wisdom of Japan
Managing for Total Quality Control
Hajime Karatsu,

translated by David J. Lu

As productivity goes up, the cost of quality comes down. And as quality improves, the cost to produce comes down. Karatsu, winner of a Deming Prize who has been involved with the quality movement in Japan since its inception, discusses the purpose and techniques of Total Quality Control (TQC), how it differs from QC, and why it is so effective. There is no better introduction to TQC than this book; essential reading for all American managers.
ISBN 0-915299-18-6 / 152 pages / $34.95 / Order code WISD-BK

TQM for Technical Groups
Applying the Principles of Total Quality to Product Development

Bunteru Kurahara, Kiyoshi Uchimaru, and Susumu Okamoto

This practical book provides a new perspective especially for technical groups working to achieve total quality in product development. Written in two parts, it first details the application of TQM methods to product design at NEC IC Microcomputer Systems, winner of the 1987 Deming Prize. It then addresses the process of TQM implementation in technical groups with emphasis on the role of corporate management and policy deployment (hoshin kanri). The case study provides an inside look at the trials, errors, and ultimate success of NEC's TQM program.
ISBN 1-56327-005-6 / 224 pages / $59.95 / Order code TQMTQ-BK

Poka-Yoke
Improving Product Quality by Preventing Defects

compiled by Nikkan Kogyo Shimbun, Ltd./Factory Magazine (ed.)
preface by Shigeo Shingo

If your goal is 100% zero defects, here is the book for you — a completely illustrated guide to poka-yoke (mistake-proofing) for supervisors and shop-floor workers. Many poka-yoke devices come from line workers and are implemented with the help of engineering staff. The result is better product quality — and greater participation by workers in efforts to improve your processes, your products, and your company as a whole.
ISBN 0-915299-31-3 / 288 pages / $59.95 / Order code IPOKA-BK

Achieving Total Quality Management
A Program for Action

Michel Perigord

This is an outstanding book on total quality management (TQM) — a compact guide to the concepts, methods, and techniques involved in achieving total quality. It shows you how to make TQM a company-wide strategy, not just in technical areas, but in marketing and administration as well. Written in an accessible, instructive style by a top European quality expert, it is methodical, logical, and thorough. An historical outline and discussion of the quality-price relationship, is followed by an investigation of the five quality imperatives (conformity, prevention, excellence, measurement, and responsibility). Major methods and tools for total quality are spelled out and implementation strategies are reviewed.
ISBN 0-915299-60-7 / 384 pages / $45.00 / Order Code ACHTQM-BK

Productivity Press, Inc., Dept. BK, P.O. Box 3007, Cambridge, MA 02140 1-800-274-9911

COMPLETE LIST OF TITLES FROM PRODUCTIVITY PRESS

Akao, Yoji (ed.). **Quality Function Deployment: Integrating Customer Requirements into Product Design**
ISBN 0-915299-41-0 / 1990 / 387 pages / $ 75.00 / order code QFD

Akiyama, Kaneo. **Function Analysis: Systematic Improvement of Quality and Performance**
ISBN 0-915299-81-X / 1991 / 288 pages / $59.95 / order code FA

Asaka, Tetsuichi and Kazuo Ozeki (eds.). **Handbook of Quality Tools: The Japanese Approach**
ISBN 0-915299-45-3 / 1990 / 336 pages / $59.95 / order code HQT

Belohlav, James A. **Championship Management: An Action Model for High Performance**
ISBN 0-915299-76-3 / 1990 / 265 pages / $29.95 / order code CHAMPS

Birkholz, Charles and Jim Villella. **The Battle to Stay Competitive: Changing the Traditional Workplace**
ISBN 0-915299-96-8 / 1991 / 110 pages paper / $9.95 /order code BATTLE

Christopher, William F. **Productivity Measurement Handbook**
ISBN 0-915299-05-4 / 1985 / 680 pages / $137.95 / order code PMH

D'Egidio, Franco. **The Service Era: Leadership in a Global Environment**
ISBN 0-915299-68-2 / 1990 / 165 pages / $29.95 / order code SERA

Ford, Henry. **Today and Tomorrow**
ISBN 0-915299-36-4 / 1988 / 286 pages / $24.95 / order code FORD

Fukuda, Ryuji. **CEDAC: A Tool for Continuous Systematic Improvement**
ISBN 0-915299-26-7 / 1990 / 144 pages / $49.95 / order code CEDAC

Fukuda, Ryuji. **Managerial Engineering: Techniques for Improving Quality and Productivity in the Workplace** (rev.)
ISBN 0-915299-09-7 / 1986 / 208 pages / $39.95 / order code ME

Gotoh, Fumio. **Equipment Planning for TPM: Maintenance Prevention Design**
ISBN 0-915299-77-1 / 1991 / 320 pages / $75.00 / order code ETPM

Greif, Michel. **The Visual Factory: Building Participation Through Shared Information**
ISBN 0-915299-67-4 / 1991 / 320 pages / $49.95 / order code VFAC

Hatakeyama, Yoshio. **Manager Revolution! A Guide to Survival in Today's Changing Workplace**
ISBN 0-915299-10-0 / 1986 / 208 pages / $24.95 / order code MREV

Hirano, Hiroyuki. **JIT Factory Revolution: A Pictorial Guide to Factory Design of the Future**
ISBN 0-915299-44-5 / 1989 / 227 pages / $49.95 / order code JITFAC

Hirano, Hiroyuki. **JIT Implementation Manual: The Complete Guide to Just-In-Time Manufacturing**
ISBN 0-915299-66-6 / 1990 / 1006 pages / $2500.00 / order code HIRJIT

Horovitz, Jacques. **Winning Ways: Achieving Zero-Defect Service**
ISBN 0-915299-78-X / 1990 / 165 pages / $24.95 / order code WWAYS

Ishiwata, Junichi. **IE for the Shop Floor: Productivity Through Process Analysis**
ISBN 0-915299-82-8 / 1991 / 208 pages / $39.95 / order code SHOPF1

Japan Human Relations Association (ed.). **The Idea Book: Improvement Through TEI (Total Employee Involvement)**
ISBN 0-915299-22-4 / 1988 / 232 pages / $49.95 / order code IDEA

Japan Human Relations Association (ed.). **The Service Industry Idea Book: Employee Involvement in Retail and Office Improvement**
ISBN 0-915299-65-8 / 1991 / 294 pages / $49.95 / order code SIDEA

Japan Management Association (ed.). **Kanban and Just-In-Time at Toyota: Management Begins at the Workplace** (rev.), Translated by David J. Lu
ISBN 0-915299-48-8 / 1989 / 224 pages / $36.50 / order code KAN

Japan Management Association and Constance E. Dyer. **The Canon Production System: Creative Involvement of the Total Workforce**
ISBN 0-915299-06-2 / 1987 / 251 pages / $36.95 / order code CAN

Jones, Karen (ed.). **The Best of TEI: Current Perspectives on Total Employee Involvement**
ISBN 0-915299-63-1 / 1989 / 502 pages / $175.00 / order code TEI

JUSE. **TQC Solutions: The 14-Step Process**
ISBN 0-915299-79-8 / 1991 / 416 pages / 2 volumes / $120.00 / order code TQCS

Kanatsu, Takashi. **TQC for Accounting: A New Role in Companywide Improvement**
ISBN 0-915299-73-9 / 1991 / 244 pages / $45.00 / order code TQCA

Karatsu, Hajime. **Tough Words For American Industry**
ISBN 0-915299-25-9 / 1988 / 178 pages / $24.95 / order code TOUGH

Karatsu, Hajime. **TQC Wisdom of Japan: Managing for Total Quality Control**, Translated by David J. Lu
ISBN 0-915299-18-6 / 1988 / 136 pages / $34.95 / order code WISD

Kato, Kenichiro. **I.E. for the Shop Floor: Productivity Through Motion Study**
ISBN 1-56327-000-5 / 1991 / 224 pages / $39.95 / order code SHOPF2

Kaydos, Will. **Measuring, Managing, and Maximizing Performance**
ISBN 0-915299- 98-4 / 1991 / 304 pages / $34.95 / order code MMMP

Kobayashi, Iwao. **20 Keys to Workplace Improvement**
ISBN 0-915299-61-5 / 1990 / 264 pages / $34.95 / order code 20KEYS

Lu, David J. **Inside Corporate Japan: The Art of Fumble-Free Management**
ISBN 0-915299-16-X / 1987 / 278 pages / $24.95 / order code ICJ

Maskell, Brian H. **Performance Measurement for World Class Manufacturing: A Model for American Companies**
ISBN 0-915299-99-2 / 1991 / 448 pages / $49.95 / order code PERFM

Merli, Giorgio. **Co-makership: The New Supply Strategy for Manufacturers**
ISBN 0915299-84-4 / 1991 / 224 pages / $39.95 / order code COMAKE

Merli, Giorgio. **Total Manufacturing Management: Production Organization for the 1990s**
ISBN 0-915299-58-5 / 1990 / 224 pages / $39.95 / order code TMM

Mizuno, Shigeru (ed.). **Management for Quality Improvement: The 7 New QC Tools**
ISBN 0-915299-29-1 / 1988 / 324 pages / $59.95 / order code 7QC

Monden, Yasuhiro and Michiharu Sakurai (eds.). **Japanese Management Accounting: A World Class Approach to Profit Management**
ISBN 0-915299-50-X / 1990 / 568 pages / $59.95 / order code JMACT

Productivity Press, Inc., Dept. BK, P.O. Box 3007, Cambridge, MA 02140 1-800-274-9911

Nachi-Fujikoshi (ed.). **Training for TPM: A Manufacturing Success Story**
ISBN 0-915299-34-8 / 1990 / 272 pages / $59.95 / order code CTPM

Nakajima, Seiichi. **Introduction to TPM: Total Productive Maintenance**
ISBN 0-915299-23-2 / 1988 / 149 pages / $45.00 / order code ITPM

Nakajima, Seiichi. **TPM Development Program: Implementing Total Productive Maintenance**
ISBN 0-915299-37-2 / 1989 / 428 pages / $85.00 / order code DTPM

Nikkan Kogyo Shimbun, Ltd./Factory Magazine (ed.). **Poka-yoke: Improving Product Quality by Preventing Defects**
ISBN 0-915299-31-3 / 1989 / 288 pages / $59.95 / order code IPOKA

Nikkan Kogyo Shimbun/Esme McTighe (ed.). **Factory Management Notebook Series: Mixed Model Production**
ISBN 0-915299-97-6 / 1991 / 184 / $125.00 / order code N1-MM

Nikkan Kogyo Shimbun/Esme McTighe (ed.). **Factory Management Notebook Series: Visual Control Systems**
ISBN 0-915299-54-2 / 1991 / 194 pages / $125.00 / order code N1-VCS

Nikkan Kogyo Shimbun/Esme McTighe (ed.). **Factory Management Notebook Series: Autonomation/Automation**
ISBN 0-0-56327-002-1 / 1991 / 200 pages / $125.00 / order code N1-AA

Ohno, Taiichi. **Toyota Production System: Beyond Large-Scale Production**
ISBN 0-915299-14-3 / 1988 / 162 pages / $39.95 / order code OTPS

Ohno, Taiichi. **Workplace Management**
ISBN 0-915299-19-4 / 1988 / 165 pages / $34.95 / order code WPM

Ohno, Taiichi and Setsuo Mito. **Just-In-Time for Today and Tomorrow**
ISBN 0-915299-20-8 / 1988 / 208 pages / $34.95 / order code OMJIT

Perigord, Michel. **Achieving Total Quality Management: A Program for Action**
ISBN 0-915299-60-7 / 1991 / 384 pages / $45.00 / order code ACHTQM

Psarouthakis, John. **Better Makes Us Best**
ISBN 0-915299-56-9 / 1989 / 112 pages / $16.95 / order code BMUB

Robinson, Alan. **Continuous Improvement in Operations: A Systematic Approach to Waste Reduction**
ISBN 0-915299-51-8 / 1991 / 416 pages / $34.95 / order code ROB2-C

Robson, Ross (ed.). **The Quality and Productivity Equation: American Corporate Strategies for the 1990s**
ISBN 0-915299-71-2 / 1990 / 558 pages / $29.95 / order code QPE

Shetty, Y.K and Vernon M. Buehler (eds.). **Competing Through Productivity and Quality**
ISBN 0-915299-43-7 / 1989 / 576 pages / $39.95 / order code COMP

Shingo, Shigeo. **Non-Stock Production: The Shingo System for Continuous Improvement**
ISBN 0-915299-30-5 / 1988 / 480 pages / $75.00 / order code NON

Shingo, Shigeo. **A Revolution In Manufacturing: The SMED System**, Translated by Andrew P. Dillon
ISBN 0-915299-03-8 / 1985 / 383 pages / $70.00 / order code SMED

Shingo, Shigeo. **The Sayings of Shigeo Shingo: Key Strategies for Plant Improvement**, Translated by Andrew P. Dillon
ISBN 0-915299-15-1 / 1987 / 208 pages / $39.95 / order code SAY

Shingo, Shigeo. **A Study of the Toyota Production System from an Industrial Engineering Viewpoint**
ISBN 0-915299-17-8 / 1989 / 293 pages / $39.95 / order code STREV

Shingo, Shigeo. **Zero Quality Control: Source Inspection and the Poka-yoke System**, Translated by Andrew P. Dillon
ISBN 0-915299-07-0 / 1986 / 328 pages / $70.00 / order code ZQC

Shinohara, Isao (ed.). **New Production System: JIT Crossing Industry Boundaries**
ISBN 0-915299-21-6 / 1988 / 224 pages / $34.95 / order code NPS

Sugiyama, Tomo. **The Improvement Book: Creating the Problem-Free Workplace**
ISBN 0-915299-47-X / 1989 / 236 pages / $49.95 / order code IB

Suzue, Toshio and Akira Kohdate. **Variety Reduction Program (VRP): A Production Strategy for Product Diversification**
ISBN 0-915299-32-1 / 1990 / 164 pages / $59.95 / order code VRP

Tateisi, Kazuma. **The Eternal Venture Spirit: An Executive's Practical Philosophy**
ISBN 0-915299-55-0 / 1989 / 208 pages/ $19.95 / order code EVS

Yasuda, Yuzo. **40 Years, 20 Million Ideas: The Toyota Suggestion System**
ISBN 0-915299-74-7 / 1991 / 210 pages / $39.95 / order code 4020

Audio-Visual Programs

Japan Management Association. **Total Productive Maintenance: Maximizing Productivity and Quality**
ISBN 0-915299-46-1 / 167 slides / 1989 / $749.00 / order code STPM
ISBN 0-915299-49-6 / 2 videos / 1989 / $749.00 / order code VTPM

Shingo, Shigeo. **The SMED System**, Translated by Andrew P. Dillon
ISBN 0-915299-11-9 / 181 slides / 1986 / $749.00 / order code S5
ISBN 0-915299-27-5 / 2 videos / 1987 / $749.00 / order code V5

Shingo, Shigeo. **The Poka-yoke System**, Translated by Andrew P. Dillon
ISBN 0-915299-13-5 / 235 slides / 1987 / $749.00 / order code S6
ISBN 0-915299-28-3 / 2 videos / 1987 / $749.00 / order code V6

Returns of AV programs willl be accepted for incorrect or damaged shipments only.

TO ORDER: Write, phone, or fax Productivity Press, Dept. BK, P.O. Box 3007, Cambridge, MA 02140, phone 1-800-274-9911, fax 617-864-6286. Send check or charge to your credit card (American Express, Visa, MasterCard accepted).

U.S. ORDERS: Add $5 shipping for first book, $2 each additional for UPS surface delivery. CT residents add 8% and MA residents 5% sales tax. For each AV program that you order, add $5 for programs with 1 or 2 tapes, and $12 for programs with 3 or more tapes.

INTERNATIONAL ORDERS: Write, phone, or fax for quote and indicate shipping method desired. Pre-payment in U.S. dollars must accompany your order (checks must be drawn on U.S. banks). When quote is returned with payment, your order will be shipped promptly by the method requested.

NOTE: Prices subject to change without notice.